Essential
Laboratory
Mathematics

Concepts and Applications
for the Chemical and Clinical
Laboratory Technician

PUBLISHING

Developmental Editor: Wendy Thompson
Copy Editor: Maura McMillan

ISBN 1-56930-056-9

Typesetting: Saxon and Associates, Inc.

SKIDMORE-ROTH PUBLISHING, INC.
2620 S. Parker Road, #147
Aurora, Colorado 80014
800-825-3150

ACKNOWLEDGMENTS

Thanks to Lyn, Courtney, and Chris Timmons and Rob, Bobby and Tyler Johnson for their support and patience with us throughout this project. Without the support of our families, this book would not have been possible. We would also like to acknowledge and thank our friends and colleagues at Alamance Community College who gave us advice, input, and information for this book: Peggy Simpson, Chairman of Medical Laboratory Technology Program; William H. Woodruff, Chairman of the Biotechnology Program; Bonnie Ramey, Instructor in the Mathematics Department; Pam Hall and Dana Lunday, Instructors in the MLT Program; and Vickie Whitaker at the NC State Laboratory of Public Health.

PREFACE

The purpose of this textbook is to provide a mathematics textbook for the student beginning the study of clinical laboratory sciences. We have tried to present clear explanations of the mathematical calculations needed in the chemistry laboratory. Each chapter is divided into sections with practice problems provided at the end of each section for immediate practice. At the end of each chapter is a Chapter Summary containing important terms and formulas to remember. A set of Review Problems is also provided at the end of each chapter as a cumulative exercise. Mathematics is a skill that requires adequate practice, so we have tried to provide plenty of opportunities for students to practice and refine their mathematical skills and understanding.

An explanation of the use of calculators in certain operations is provided when necessary. For example, logarithms, which are used to calculate the pH of solutions, are derived today using calculators instead of logarithmic tables. In the Appendix, we have included a brief explanation of the basic calculator functions a chemistry student should know. This introduction to the scientific calculator is designed to help students who may not be familiar with all of the functions on a scientific calculator.

Suggested laboratory activities are provided at the end of most of the chapters. These activities are designed to be easily done by beginning students. They should be used by the instructor to help reinforce the concepts presented in each chapter.

Our goal was to write a mathematics textbook that could be easily understood by students of laboratory science. We have tried to provide clear, straightforward explanations with examples throughout the text. We hope that you will find our approach helpful in your studies of the mathematics of the laboratory. If anyone wishes to offer suggestions, criticisms, or has questions, please feel free to contact us directly at Alamance Community College, PO Box 8000, Graham, NC, 27253-8000, (e-mail: timmonsd@alamance.cc.nc.us or johnsonc@alamance.cc.nc.us), or through the publisher.

Catherine Johnson and Daniel Timmons

TABLE OF CONTENTS

In This Chapter:

The mathematical topics presented in this chapter are some of the basic mathematical concepts and processes that are used in the calculations required when doing experiments or testing procedures in a laboratory. A good understanding of calculations involving percent, ratio and proportion, measurements and scientific notation is vital for the student's continued success in this area of study.

1.1 PERCENT

Percent means "per hundred". Any number given as a percent (%) means that many parts per 100 parts. For example, 5% means 5 parts per 100 parts which can also be written 5/100 or 0.05.

In working with problems involving percents, some conversions of % to decimals or fractions may be needed. Review the following rules.

1. <u>Changing % to fraction</u> - Remove the % sign, multiply the number by 1/100. Reduce the fraction.

$$6\% = 6 \times \frac{1}{100} = \frac{6}{100} = \frac{3}{50}$$

$$33\tfrac{1}{3}\,\% = 33\tfrac{1}{3} \times \frac{1}{100} = \frac{100}{3} \times \frac{1}{100} = \frac{1}{3}$$

2. <u>Changing % to a decimal</u> - Remove the % sign and multiply the number by 0.01. (This is the same as moving the decimal two places to the left.)

$$6\% = 6 \times 0.01 = 0.06$$

$$150\% = 150 \times 0.01 = 1.5$$

3. <u>Changing fraction
or decimal to %</u> - Multiply the fraction or decimal by 100 and add a % sign.

$$\text{fraction to } \% : \quad \frac{3}{50} \times 100 = \frac{300}{50} = 6\%$$

$$\text{decimal to } \% : \quad 0.06 \times 100 = 6\%$$

✎ **Note:** Many times it is easier to change a fraction to a % by first changing it to a decimal number and then multiplying it by 100. This is especially true when using a calculator for these conversions.

$$3/4 = (3 \div 4) \times 100 = 0.75 \times 100 = 75\%$$

Remember that the % sign is very important in determining the value of the number. The percent symbol means "out of one hundred".

$$0.05 = 5\% = 5/100 \; (\; 5 \text{ out of } 100 \;)$$
$$0.05\% = 0.05/100 = 5/10000 \; (0.05 \text{ out of } 100 \text{ or } 5 \text{ out of } 10000)$$

Percents are commonly used in expressing the concentration of solutions that you will work with or mix in a laboratory. For example, a 10% salt solution usually means 10 g of salt in 100 ml of solution. However, a 10% salt solution could also mean 10 g of salt in 100 g of total solution. Therefore, the units of measure implied by a % must be specified as weight per unit volume, volume per unit volume, or weight per unit weight. Specifically, we define the following ratios:

$$x \, \%^{w/v} = \frac{x \text{ g solute}}{100 \text{ ml total solution}}$$

$$x \, \%^{v/v} = \frac{x \text{ ml liquid solute}}{100 \text{ ml total solution}}$$

$$x \, \%^{w/w} = \frac{x \text{ g solute}}{100 \text{ g total solution}}$$

Therefore, a $10\%^{w/v}$ salt solution contains 10 g of salt in 100 ml of solution. A $10\%^{w/w}$ salt solution contains 10 g of salt in 100 g of total solution.

The making of a solution using a weight/weight mixture is the most accurate method of the three because mass does not vary with temperature as does volume. If a very accurate and precise measurement of concentration is needed, particularly for the concentration of a solid in a solid, this method is employed. However, it is the least used method for laboratory work. Most solutions created in a laboratory will be weight/volume mixtures (if the solute is a solid) or volume/volume mixtures (if the solute is a liquid). The volume/volume mixture is the least accurate since liquids are easily affected by changes in temperature. However, if care is taken, the amount of variation can be minimized and will then be acceptable for a particular use of a solution.

NOTES

NOTES

In laboratory work, you may be asked to give the concentration of a solution in the form of a percent. This percent can be found by setting up a ratio of parts of solute to total volume and converting the fraction to a percent using the above rules.

Example 1.1: Give the concentration of a solution in percent form if the solution contains 25 parts solute in 80 parts total solution.

Solution: Set up a fraction relating the parts and use rule 3 to convert it to a %. Either method that you use for conversion of the fraction to a % will give the correct percent concentration. Remember when setting up the ratio that the denominator always represents the total volume of the solution.

Method A: $\dfrac{25 \text{ parts}}{80 \text{ parts}} \times 100 = \dfrac{2500}{80} = 31.25\%$

Method B:
$\dfrac{25 \text{ parts}}{80 \text{ parts}} = (25 \div 80) \times 100 = 0.3125 \times 100 = 31.25\%$

Therefore, a solution containing 25 parts solute in 80 parts solution has a concentration of 31.25%.

Example 1.2: Give the % concentration of a solution containing 5 ml of alcohol mixed with 20 ml of water.

Solution: This solution contains 5 ml of alcohol out of 25 ml total solution. Therefore, convert the fraction 5/25 to a %.

$$\dfrac{5}{25} = (5 \div 25) \times 100 = 0.2 \times 100 = 20\%$$

Therefore, a solution of 5 ml of alcohol mixed with 20 ml of water results in a solution which has a concentration of $20\%^{v/v}$

Practice Problem Set 1.1:

1. Change each percent to a fraction. Reduce it to lowest terms.

   a. 85%

   b. 8%

   c. 16 1/2%

   d. 125%

   e. 1/4%

   f. 66⅔ %

2. Change each % to an equivalent decimal.

   a. 5%

   b. 75%

   c. 1.5%

   d. 12 1/2%

   e. 0.04%

   f. 115%

3. Change each fraction or decimal to a %.

   a. 3/4

   b. 3/8

   c. 2/3

   d. 0.005

   e. 1.2

   f. 0.625

4. State each of the following as a percent:

   a. 15 parts in 100 total parts

   b. 8 parts in 10 total parts

   c. 100 total parts containing 15.5 parts solute

   d. 0.01 parts in 100 total parts

   e. 1 part in 3 total parts

   f. 0.025 parts in 50 total parts

5. What would be the concentration of a salt solution which contains 15 g of salt in 250 ml of water? (Be sure to label the answer with v/v, w/v, or w/w.)

NOTES

6. Ten milliliters of ethanol are mixed with 70 ml of water. What is the concentration of the resulting solution?

7. Five grams of a solute are mixed with a solvent resulting in a solution which weighs 15 grams. Give the % concentration of this solution.

8. Explain the difference between a $10\%^{w/v}$ salt solution and a $10\%^{w/w}$ salt solution.

1.2 SCIENTIFIC NOTATION

Very large and very small numbers are encountered in the natural sciences and therefore in laboratory work. For example, the concentration of hydrogen ions in water is 0.0000001 moles per liter. To handle numbers that involve a large number of zeroes, a more convenient system called **scientific notation** has been devised. In this system, numbers are expressed using powers of 10.

To express a number in scientific notation, write it in the form **a × 10^n** where **a** is a number greater than or equal to one but less than 10. The value of **n** will always be an integer. If the number you are converting is greater than 10, then **n** will be a positive integer. If the number you are converting is between 0 and 1, the exponent **n** will be a negative integer. If the number you are converting is between 1 and 10, the exponent **n** will equal 0. Only positive numbers are commonly written in scientific notation.

Steps for Writing Numbers in Scientific Notation

1. Relocate the decimal to the right of the first nonzero digit.

   240,000
   2.40000
      ^

2. Count the number of places the decimal moved. This is the exponent for the 10.

   decimal moved
   5 places

3. If the number you are converting is:
   ≥ 10, exponent is positive
   < 1, exponent is negative
   1 ≤ x < 10, exponent is zero

   240,000 > 10
   so exponent
   is positive

Therefore, the number 240,000 written in correct scientific notation will be 2.4×10^5.

Example 1.3: Write each number in correct scientific notation:

$6,500 = 6.5 \times 10^3$ $0.0078 = 7.8 \times 10^{-3}$

$162 = 1.62 \times 10^2$ $7.5 = 7.5 \times 10^0$

Reverse the process when asked to change a number written in scientific notation to decimal notation.

$$7.23 \times 10^{-3} =$$
⇑　　　　⇑
1. begin with　　　2. move decimal 3 places to the left
   this number　　　　resulting in a number between 0 & 1

$$7.23 \times 10^{-3} = 0.00723$$

MULTIPLICATION IN SCIENTIFIC NOTATION

If numbers are expressed in scientific notation, they may be easily multiplied. Multiply the numbers that appear first (the values of **a** in $a \times 10^n$) and then add the powers of 10. The final answer may be expressed in correct scientific notation or as a decimal.

Example 1.4: $(6.2 \times 10^4) \times (2.1 \times 10^{-6}) =$

$$(6.2 \times 2.1) \times (10^4 \times 10^{-6}) =$$

$$13.02 \quad \times \quad 10^{4+(-6)} =$$

$$13.02 \quad \times \quad 10^{-2} =$$

Since 13.02 is greater than 10, this answer is not in correct scientific notation form. The first number should be converted to scientific notation and the resulting powers of 10 combined.

$$(1.302 \times 10^1) \quad \times \quad 10^{-2} =$$

$$1.302 \quad \times \quad 10^{-1} = 0.1302$$

DIVISION IN SCIENTIFIC NOTATION

This process is similar to multiplication except that the values of **a** are divided and the powers of 10 are subtracted. Remember the definition of subtraction of signed numbers is to subtract by adding the opposite of the number being subtracted to the first number. Therefore, the problem 4 - (-2) becomes 4 + 2 and the exponent for 10 that should appear in the final answer in the following example is 6.

Example 1.5: $(6.3 \times 10^4) \div (3 \times 10^{-2}) =$

$$(6.3 \div 3) \times (10^4 \div 10^{-2}) =$$

$$2.1 \times 10^{4-(-2)} =$$

$$2.1 \times 10^{4+2} =$$

$$2.1 \times 10^6 = 2,100,000$$

USING CALCULATORS TO DO SCIENTIFIC NOTATION*

Many calculators have a mode that will enable you to do calculations exclusively in scientific notation. However, when doing problems which include some numbers in decimal notation and others in scientific notation, the numbers expressed in scientific notation can be entered into the calculator using the EXP button (or the EE button) on most calculators. This button tells the calculator that the number you are entering into the calculator is in scientific notation. Follow these steps to enter the number 6.5×10^{-2}.

Enter: 6.5 | EXP | 2 | +/- |

The display should look like this:

| -02 |
| 6.5 |

The -02 is the exponent for the 10 which is already programmed into the calculator and does not appear on your screen.

To multiply two numbers that are expressed in scientific notation using a calculator, look at the following example.

Example 1.6: $(6.5 \times 10^{-2}) \times (1.053 \times 10^4) =$

Enter   6.5 | EXP | 2 | +/- | | × | 1.053 | EXP | 4 | = | 684.45

✎ **AN IMPORTANT NOTE:** Do not enter the number 10 when using your calculator to do scientific notation. If you enter a 10 while using the | EXP | button, this will change the value of the exponent and cause the answer to be incorrect.

NOTES

NOTES

The answers to these problems may or may not be expressed in scientific notation depending upon the number of digits in the answer. If an answer is displayed in scientific notation on your calculator, remember to write it in standard form when giving your final answer. For example, $3.5 \ ^{-04}$ should be written 3.5×10^{-4}. If you want all of your answers to be expressed in scientific notation, the calculator should be put into scientific notation mode according to the directions that accompany your specific make of calculator.

*Individual calculators may vary in method. See your instruction manual for complete instructions.

Practice Problem Set 1.2:

1. Write each number in scientific notation.

   a. 6,500   d. 196,000,000

   b. 0.00253   e. 0.0000015

   c. 1734.8   f. 3.8

2. Write each number in decimal notation.

   a. 6.5×10^{-2} e. 3×10^{-5}

   b. 4.135×10^{4} f. 7.89×10^{0}

   c. 7.02×10^{3} g. 6.001×10^{2}

   d. 4.1×10^{-1}

3. Do the following problems involving scientific notation.
   Express each of the final answers in correct scientific notation.

   a. $(3.8 \times 10^{-2}) \times (4.15 \times 10^{8})$

   b. $(7.5 \times 10^{4}) \times (2.10 \times 10^{5})$

   c. $(9.21 \times 10^{-3}) \div (8.15 \times 10^{-1})$

   d. $(7.4 \times 10^{4}) \div (2 \times 10^{5})$

   e. $\dfrac{(6.5 \times 10^{-1}) \times (3.02 \times 10^{4})}{2.5 \times 10^{8}}$

   f. $\dfrac{(3.5 \times 10^{4}) \times (2.6 \times 10^{-2})}{(1.0054 \times 10^{6})}$

   g. $\dfrac{(2.067 \times 10^{-3}) \times (9.8 \times 10^{-2})}{(4.01 \times 10^{4})}$

NOTES

NOTES

1.3 SIGNIFICANT FIGURES

The result of any measurement is expressed using a numerical value together with a unit of that measurement. For example,

$$\overset{\text{measurement unit}}{\underset{\text{numerical value}}{\underset{\Downarrow}{64.5 \text{ ml} \ = \ 0.0645 \ \text{L}}}{\overset{\Uparrow}{}}}$$

Numbers obtained from a measurement are **approximate** values. There is always some uncertainty due to the limitations of the measuring devices used and the skill of the individual making the measurement. The figures used to report a result should reflect the precision of the test and sensitivity of the measuring device that produced the value. To express this precision, the number should contain all the digits that are known plus one digit that is estimated. These are the **significant figures** (or significant digits). For instance, a measurement described by the number 2.54 can be supposed to have an actual value greater than or equal to 2.535 but less than or equal to 2.544. By simply writing 2.54, we indicate our uncertainty about exactly where in that range the measurement falls. Our measurement is precise to 3 significant figures.

Some numbers are **exact** and occur in simple counting operations. For example, you can count exactly 25 oranges. Defined numbers such as 12 inches = 1 foot are also considered to be exact. Significant figures are used for measured values, not counted or exact values.

Rules for Determining Significant Figures

1. In any measurement, all nonzero numbers are significant.

2. Zeroes may or may not be significant as follows:

    a. Zeroes between nonzero digits are significant.

    > 7005 has 4 significant figures
    > 6.0035 has 5 significant figures

b. Zeroes on the right hand end of a number that include a decimal point are significant.

> 13.500 has 5 significant figures
> 41.0 has 3 significant figures
> 60. has 2 significant figures

c. Zeroes that precede that first nonzero digit in a decimal number are <u>not</u> significant. These zeroes are used to locate the decimal point.

> 0.0083 has 2 significant figures (8, 3)
> 0.0103 has 3 significant figures (1, 0, 3)

d. Zeroes at the end of a number without a decimal are considered ambiguous and are <u>not</u> significant.

> 5000 has 1 significant figure (5)
> 350 has 2 significant figures (3, 5)

In the event that a whole number contains zeroes that are significant, a bar is placed over the rightmost significant zero. For example, if there are two significant figures in the number 5000, it would be written as 5$\bar{0}$00. The numbers to the right of the $\bar{0}$ are not significant. The number 500$\bar{0}$0 would have 4 significant figures.

In calculations we often obtain answers that have more digits than we are justified in using. When digits are dropped from a number, the value of the last digit retained is determined by a process known as **rounding off numbers**. Two rules will be used in this book for rounding off numbers.

Rules for Rounding Off Numbers

Rule 1: When the first digit after those you want to retain is 4 or less, that digit and all others to its right are dropped. The last digit retained is not changed.

For example,

> 74.593 rounds off to 74.59 (the 3 is dropped)
> 3.00249 rounds off to 3.002 (the 4 & 9 are both dropped)

NOTES

NOTES

Rule 2: When the first digit after those you want to retain is 5 or greater, that digit and all others to the right of it are dropped and the last digit retained is increased by one.

For example,

1.0268 rounds off to 1.027
(the 8 is dropped and the 6 increased to a 7)

Numbers that are the result of a measurement should be rounded to the correct number of significant figures using these rules for rounding. Exact numbers do not need to be rounded to significant figures since they are not approximate.

SIGNIFICANT FIGURES IN CALCULATIONS

The results of a calculation based on measurements cannot be more precise than the measurements used to achieve that result. Because of the arithmetic rules for the placement of decimals in multiplication and division problems, answers may seem to be more precise than they actually are. Therefore, in calculations involving multiplication or division of measured amounts, the answer should contain the same number of significant figures as in the measurement that has the least number of significant figures. For example, the product shown on a calculator when multiplying 2.54×3.213 is 8.16102. However, the most accurate value we can give for the answer is 8.16 because the least precise factor (2.54) has only 3 significant figures.

Rule for Multiplying/Dividing Measurements

When multiplying or dividing measurements having differing numbers of digits, the answer should have the same number of digits as the measurement with the least number of significant figures.

Example 1.7: Multiply the following measured amounts and round the answer to the correct number of significant figures.

$$\frac{(0.0211)(2.53)(13.82)}{1200}$$

The calculated result is 0.000614794.

Examine the individual factors to determine rounding:

0.0211 has 3 significant figures
2.53 has 3 significant figures
13.82 has 4 significant figures
1200 has 2 significant figures

The factor 1200 contains the least number of significant figures (2) and therefore the calculated answer should be rounded to two significant figures.

The correctly rounded answer is **0.00061**.

The results of addition or subtraction of measurements must be expressed to the same precision at the least precise measurement. The answer should contain no more digits to the right of the decimal point than are contained in the quantity that has the least number of digits to the right of the decimal point. For example, 6.53 g + 12.8 g = 19.33 g when added on a calculator. However, to avoid an answer that appears more precise than the original problem allows, the final answer should be reported as 19.3 g.

Rule for Addition/Subtraction of Measurements

In adding or subtracting measured amounts the final answer should be only as precise as (that is, contain the same number of decimal places as) the least precise measurement in the problem.

Example 1.8: Add 125.17 g, 129.2 g and 52.24 g rounding the answer appropriately.

```
  125.17 g   (precise to 2 decimal places)
  129.2  g   (precise to 1 decimal place)
+  52.24 g   (precise to 2 decimal places)
  306.61 g   rounds to 306.6 g (precise to 1 decimal place)
```

If a chain calculation is done where several operations are needed, rounding should be done only on the final answer. Base this rounding on the significant digits of the measurements given in the problem before they were combined.

NOTES

Measurements that are being added, subtracted, multiplied or divided must be expressed in the same units before being combined. In a problem such as 2.5 g + 35 mg, the grams must be converted to milligrams (or milligrams to grams) before the addition is done. Methods for the conversions of measurement units will be discussed in the section 1.5.

Practice Problem Set 1.3:

1. How many significant figures are in each of the following measurements?

    a. 4.8 cm

    b. 350 ml

    c. 0.0005 mg

    d. 5.420 mm

    e. 950.6 µg

    f. 6.002 L

    g. 15.0 g

    h. 0.001 m

    i. 1700. km

    j. 205 m

2. Do the following problems rounding each answer to the correct number of significant figures. Assume all numbers are measurements.

    a. $134 \times 26 =$

    b. $14.0 \div 5.3 =$

    c. $1.64 + 23.3 - 0.0034 =$

    d. $8.2 + 0.25 =$

    e. $\dfrac{(160)(3.3)}{6} =$

    f. $\dfrac{(17.5)(2.002)}{3.3} =$

3. Suppose that you measured the sides of a triangle with a ruler and found their lengths to be 6.00 in., 3.82 in. and 5.439 in. What would the perimeter of the triangle be?

4. If the average weight of a penny is 6.25 g, then how much do 10 of them weigh?

NOTES

5. The area of a triangle is easily found with the formula
    A = ½ bh. If the base length is measured to be 35.45 cm
    and the height is measured as 3.62 cm, what is the area of
    the triangle?

6. Three bags of chocolate candies are weighed on scales of
    differing sensitivities. The results are 47.8 g, 47.95 g, and
    47.925 g. Find the average weight of the three bags.

1.4 RATIO/PROPORTION

A **ratio** is an amount of one thing relative to another - a comparison of 2 values. A ratio considers the relative size of two numbers. Ratios may be expressed in the following ways:

1) as a fraction such as 4/5

2) using the ratio symbol (:) such as 4:5

3) using the word "to" and stating the ratio as 4 to 5

A ratio should be written exactly as the words expressing it are written. A ratio of 2 parts serum to 5 parts saline would be written 2/5 or 2:5. A ratio of serum to total volume would be 2/7 or 2:7 since 2 parts serum + 5 parts saline = 7 parts total volume.

Proportions are equal ratios. They represent two ratios that have the same relative meaning but different amounts. For example, the ratio 1:4 is the same ratio as 3:12. Therefore the proportion 1:4::3:12 (read "one is to four as three is to twelve") is true because the two ratios equal each other. The easiest way to solve a proportion is to write it in fraction form. The proportion 1:4::3:12 is written $\frac{1}{4} = \frac{3}{12}$.

To solve a proportion, we use the property of proportions that states:

The cross products of any true proportion are equal.

We can see that this property is true by looking at the above example and noting that $1 \times 12 = 3 \times 4$.

NOTES

Example 1.9: Solve the following proportion using the property of cross products.

$$\frac{x}{8} = \frac{30}{24}$$

$$24x = (8)(30) \quad \text{(cross products)}$$

$$24x = 240$$

$$x = \frac{240}{24}$$

$$x = 10$$

Therefore, when x = 10, the proportion is true.

In a laboratory, if a different volume of a solution is to be made **without changing the concentration**, the ratio and proportion method will probably be used. Three of the four values must be known, however. Set the given ratio equal to the unknown ratio and use the property of cross products to solve for the missing value. Be sure the given ratio and the unknown ratio are written in the same order and are in the same units.

Example 1.10: If there are 4 g of solute in 15 ml of solution, how many grams would be in 75 ml of this solution?

Solution: Given ratio is $\dfrac{4 \text{ g}}{15 \text{ ml}}$

Unknown ratio is $\dfrac{x}{75 \text{ ml}}$ (how many grams?)
                                    (in 75 ml)

Given Ratio = Unknown Ratio

$$\frac{4 \text{ g}}{15 \text{ ml}} = \frac{x}{75 \text{ ml}}$$

$(75 \text{ ml})(4 \text{ g}) \quad = \quad 15\text{x ml (cross products)}$

$300 \text{ ml g} \quad = \quad 15\text{x ml}$

$\dfrac{300 \; \cancel{\text{ml}} \; \text{g}}{15 \; \cancel{\text{ml}}} \quad = \quad \text{x (cancel like units)}$

$20 \text{ g} \quad = \quad \text{x}$

Therefore, there would be **20 g** of solute in 75 ml of solution.

Example 1.11: How much solution can be made with 8 g of solute if 2.5 g will make 20 ml?

Solution: Given ratio is $\dfrac{2.5 \text{ g}}{20 \text{ ml}}$

Unknown ratio is $\dfrac{8 \text{ g}}{\text{x}}$ (8 grams will make how much solution?)

Given Ratio = Unknown Ratio

$\dfrac{2.5 \text{ g}}{20 \text{ ml}} \quad = \quad \dfrac{8 \text{ g}}{\text{x}}$

$2.5\text{x g} \quad = \quad (8 \text{ g})(20 \text{ ml}) \text{ (cross products)}$

$2.5\text{x g} \quad = \quad 160 \text{ g ml}$

$\text{x} \quad = \quad \dfrac{160 \; \cancel{\text{g}} \; \text{ml}}{2.5 \; \cancel{\text{g}}} \quad \text{(cancel like units)}$

$\text{x} \quad = \quad 64 \text{ ml}$

Therefore, 8 g of solute will make **64 ml** of solution.

NOTES

NOTES

Practice Problem Set 1.4:

1. Tell if each of the following is a true proportion:

   a. $\dfrac{6}{7} = \dfrac{18}{21}$ b. $\dfrac{5}{6} = \dfrac{2.5}{9}$ c. $\dfrac{0.5}{8} = \dfrac{1.5}{24}$

2. Solve each of the following proportions.

   a. $x:5::21:35$ d. $9:10::4:x$

   b. $\dfrac{10}{x} = \dfrac{5}{3}$ e. $\dfrac{8}{5} = \dfrac{x}{4}$

   c. $\dfrac{2x}{7} = \dfrac{8}{14}$ f. $\dfrac{0.625}{x} = 0.25$

3. Solve each problem using a proportion.

   a. If there are 4 g of solute in 10 ml of solution, how many grams of solute would be in 75 ml of solution?

   b. If a specimen of urine contains 150 mg/100 ml of a substance, how many mg would be in 2500 ml of urine?

   c. How many grams of solute would it take to make 150 ml of solution if 5 g makes 25 ml?

   d. If 24 ml of solution are needed to prepare 36 slides for a lab test, how much solution would be needed to prepare 63 slides?

   e. A 5%$^{w/v}$ solution contains 5 g solute per 100 ml of solution. Using a proportion, determine how many milliliters of solution 7.5 g of solute will produce.

1.5 THE METRIC SYSTEM

The metric system (or SI, from Système International) is a decimal system of units for mass, length, time and other physical quantities. The system consists of one primary unit for each quantitative property and a set of prefixes used with the primary units to create larger or smaller units. These prefixes represent multiples of 10, making the metric system a decimal system of measurement. These prefixes are used with the primary units for length (meter), volume (liter), and mass (gram). When a prefix is added to a primary unit, a new unit of measure is created that has a value equal to the product of the prefix factor and the primary unit. The table that follows shows the names, values and symbols for some of these prefixes.

Table of Metric Prefixes

PREFIX	VALUE	SYMBOL
giga	10^9	G
mega	10^6	M
kilo	10^3	k
hecto	10^2	h
deka	10^1	da
-	10^0	-
deci	10^{-1}	d
centi	10^{-2}	c
milli	10^{-3}	m
micro	10^{-6}	μ
nano	10^{-9}	n

Not all of these prefixes and units will be used in laboratory work. Some of the more common units used in the laboratory include gram, milligram, microgram, nanogram, milliliter, deciliter, and millimeter.

NOTES

CONVERSIONS FROM ONE UNIT OF MEASURE TO ANOTHER

Laboratory calculations frequently involve the conversion of one unit of measure to another. For example, 250 ml may need to be converted into 0.250 liters before it can be used in a particular formula. In general, units of measure can be converted only to units of the same property. For example, units of volume (liters) cannot be converted into units of length (meters). However, all units of volume are compatible so that any unit of volume can be converted into another unit of volume.

Two methods of converting units of measure will be discussed. The use of conversion factors is one common way of changing one unit of measure into another. Another method, sometimes called "decimal bumping", uses the chart of prefixes to relocate the decimal in the number whenever a conversion is needed.

Conversion Factors

If the value of a physical quantity is given in a measurement unit that is not useful to you, a conversion of that value to its equivalent in terms of another unit may be needed. This conversion of units can be made by multiplying the original unit by an appropriate conversion factor whose value can be found from information listed in a table. A **conversion factor** is simply the ratio of a quantity stated in one unit to the same quantity stated in another unit. Thus both units will appear when the conversion factor is written out. For instance, suppose an answer stated in liters is to be converted to the answer stated in milliliters. A table will tell you that 1 liter = 1000 ml. The conversion factor will be 1000 ml/ 1 liter. The answer should be multiplied by this conversion factor so that the unwanted units cancel leaving the desired unit in the result. The following examples illustrate the use of conversion factors.

Example 1.12: Convert 0.015 L to milliliters.

We know that 1 L = 1000 ml and therefore, our conversion factor will be a ratio of these two values. The conversion factor that should be used to change liters to milliliters is 1000 ml/ 1 L since this fraction will allow us to cancel the unwanted unit (L) leaving the desired unit (ml).

$$0.015 \; \cancel{L} \; \times \; \frac{1000 \; mL}{1 \; \cancel{L}} \; = \; 15 \; mL$$

Example 1.13: Convert 250,000 meters to kilometers.

The conversion factor to change meters to kilometers is 1 km/ 1000 m.

$$250,000 \; \cancel{m} \times \; \frac{1 \; km}{1000 \; \cancel{m}} \; = \; 250 \; km$$

"Decimal Bumping"

The metric prefixes that we use are all based on powers of 10. A conversion of one unit to another, then, involves changing the given number by a power of ten. In a metric-value chart, a move from any place in the chart one place to the right changes the metric unit to the next smaller unit. In effect, the larger unit is broken down into 10 smaller units. In other words, we are multiplying the larger unit by 10 when we move one place to the right. In moving two places to the right, we are changing the larger unit by 10^2.

Likewise, a move from any place in the chart one place to the left changes the metric unit to the next larger unit. In effect, smaller units are consolidated into one larger unit 10 times larger than each smaller unit. In other words, we are dividing the smaller unit by 10 when we move one place to the left. In moving two places to the left, we are dividing the smaller by 10^2.

Look at the chart below and the examples of conversions that are given.

	K	h	da	unit	d	c	m			μ			n
	10^3	10^2	10^1	10^0	10^{-1}	10^{-2}	10^{-3}			10^{-6}			10^{-9}

NOTES

NOTES

Example 1.14: 4.29 hg = __?__ dg

Solution: Look at the chart and locate the prefix **hecto-**. Move to the right until the desired prefix **deci-** is located. This move is three places to the right; thus we move the decimal in 4.29 three places to the right adding zeroes if necessary.

Therefore, 4.29 hg = 4290 dg

Example 1.15: 15 ml = __?__ L

Solution: Look at the chart and locate the prefix **milli-**. Since **L** is a base unit, we will move from **milli-** three places to the left to the word **unit**. Therefore, we will move the decimal in 15 (understood to be located to the right of the 5) three places to the left.

Therefore, 15 ml = 0.015 L

Notice that the prefixes in the chart usually involve a change of value of 10^1 from the unit adjacent to them. However, the change between the prefixes **milli-** and **micro-** or **micro-** and **nano-** both involve a change of 10^3. This difference must be noted when counting the number of places to move the decimal. For example, changing centimeters to micrometers would involve moving the decimal four places to the right.

Example 1.16: 154 nm = __?__ mm

Solution: Locate the prefix **nano-** on the chart. The prefix **milli-** is to the left of **nano-** so the decimal will be moved to the left. Moving from **nano-** to **micro-** will move the decimal 3 places and from **micro-** to **milli-** is another 3 places. Therefore, the decimal will need to be moved a total of 6 places to the left.

Therefore, 154 nm = 0.000154 mm

Remember that when doing calculations involving several measurements, the units of measure must all be alike before the calculations can be completed. This may involve converting one unit to another before calculating.

Example 1.17: $\dfrac{(16.5 \text{ ml})(0.25 \text{ L})}{1.5 \text{ ml}}$ = ___?___ ml

Solution: Since the desired unit for the final answer is ml, all measurements in the problem itself should be converted to ml.

Therefore, 0.25 L = 250 ml ("bump" the decimal 3 places to the right)

Substituting this into the problem,

$\dfrac{(16.5 \text{ ml})(250 \text{ ml})}{1.5 \text{ ml}}$ = 2750 ml

Now, this product must be rounded to two significant figures since the least precise factors in the problem each contain 2 significant figures.

Therefore, the final answer is **2800 ml**.

NOTES

NOTES

Practice Problem Set 1.5:

1. Complete the following unit conversions.

    a. 2743 mm = __?__ m   e. 0.03 mL = __?__ L

    b. 385 g = __?__ kg   f. 0.432 km = __?__ mg

    c. 2.3 m = __?__ mm   g. 0.0088 L = __?__ mL

    d. 5470 µg = __?__ mg   h. 0.00000025 L = __?__ nl

2. How many deciliters are in 2.25 mL?

3. Fifteen liters is the same as how many centiliters?

4. Calculate and round to the correct number of significant figures.

    a. 2.5 mg + 0.383 g = __?__ g

    b. (6.5 mm)(2.85 mm) = __?__ mm^2

    c. 65.0 µg + 4.56 ng + 3.12 mg = __?__ µg

5. Convert 1.50 g/L to:

    a. mg/L

    b. mg/dl

6. Which of the following weighs the most?
    a 0.02523 kg white mouse,
    a 26530 mg brown mouse,
    or a 2.6529 × 10^{10} ng grey mouse

1.6 TEMPERATURE SCALES AND CONVERSIONS

Thermometers are calibrated so that a numerical value can be assigned to a particular temperature. This is done by defining a temperature scale. To establish a temperature scale, we may take two reference, or "fixed," points defined by physical phenomena that always occur at the same temperatures, such as, the freezing point and boiling point of water. These fixed points are the temperatures at which pure water freezes and boils under a pressure of one atmosphere (standard pressure).

THE STANDARD TEMPERATURE SCALES

There are three commonly used temperature scales. The Kelvin temperature scale and the kelvin unit are the official SI system temperature standards. The other two most common scales are the Fahrenheit and Celsius (formerly called Centigrade) scales.

The Fahrenheit temperature scale is named after Daniel Gabriel Fahrenheit (1686-1736), a German physicist who originated it and who invented the mercury-in-glass thermometer. On this common scale, the interval between the freezing and boiling points of water is divided into 180 equal steps, and the temperature is read in degrees Fahrenheit (°F). As you probably know, the freezing point of water is 32°F and the boiling point is 212°F. Room temperature is around 68°F.

The Celsius temperature scale is named after Anders C. Celsius (1701-1744), a Swedish astronomer. On this scale, the interval between the freezing and boiling points of water is divided into 100 equal steps, and the temperature is read in degrees Celsius (°C). The freezing point has a temperature of 0°C, and the boiling point a temperature of 100°C. Room temperature is around 20°C. This scale is sometimes referred to as the centigrade scale (Latin *centi*, meaning "one hundred," and German *grade*, meaning "degrees"). Oddly enough, on the original scale, the freezing point of water was taken as 100 and the boiling point 0 . The values were later reversed.

Notice that the temperature units on both scales are called *degrees*. However, the degree unit on the Celsius scale is almost twice as large as the degree unit on the Fahrenheit scale. This is due to the fact that 1 Celsius degree = 1.8 Fahrenheit degrees because the distance between the freezing and boiling points of water is 100 Celsius degrees and is 180 Fahrenheit degrees.

ABSOLUTE ZERO AND THE KELVIN SCALE

The Celsius and Fahrenheit scales are used for everyday temperature measurements. Negative temperatures that is, temperatures that register below the zero point on either of these scales are common in regions with cold climates. You may wonder how low temperature can go, that is, is there a lower limit of temperature? The answers is yes. It is determined by making measurements involving pressures and temperatures and then extrapolating the results to the *theoretically* lowest possible point. This leads to a calculated value of about -273°C or -459°F. This temperature is called *absolute zero*, and has been taken as zero point of the Kelvin temperature scale. This means that there will be no negative temperatures when measuring with the Kelvin scale since, theoretically, no temperature is possible below the zero on this scale.

The Kelvin or absolute temperature is related to the Celsius temperature by in that the size of the degrees is the same. There is a minor difference in the way that absolute temperatures are written. The term "degree" is not used nor is the degrees symbol used. So 200K is two hundred kelvins not two hundred degrees kelvin. The Kelvin scale is named after Lord Kelvin (William Thomson, 1824-1907), a British physicist.

CONVERSIONS BETWEEN TEMPERATURE SCALES

Conversion of a temperature as measured on any one of these scales can be converted into the corresponding value on any other scale by use of the following simple conversion formulas:

$$T_C = (T_F - 32)/1.8$$

$$T_F = 1.8T_C + 32$$

$$T_K = T_C + 273$$

These formulas are quick and easy to use, as the following examples will show.

Example 1.18: Change 50°F to degrees Celsius.

First choose the formula that starts with the temperature scale that you wish to switch to. In this case, that would be:

$$T_C = (T_F - 32)/1.8$$

$$T_C = (50° - 32°)1.8$$

$$T_C = 18°/1.8$$

$$T_C = 10°$$

So, 50°F = 10°C

Example 1.19: Change 30°C to degrees Fahrenheit.

$$T_F = 1.8T_C + 32$$

$$T_F = 1.8(30°) + 32°$$

$$T_F = 54° + 32°$$

$$T_F = 86°$$

So, 30°C = 86°F

Example 1.20: Change 5°C to Kelvins.

$$T_K = T_C + 273$$

$$T_K = 5 + 237$$

$$T_K = 242$$

So, 5°C = 242K

NOTES

Since negative temperatures are possible on both the Celsius and Fahrenheit scales, you will need to exercise some care in dealing with the formulas whenever temperatures are at or below the freezing point of water. Here some examples with lower temperatures.

Example 1.21: Change 14°F to degrees Celsius.

$$T_C = (T_F - 32)/1.8$$

$$T_C = (14° - 32°)/1.8$$

$$T_C = (-18°)/1.8$$

$$T_C = -10°$$

Thus, 14°F = -10°C

Example 1.22: Change -55°C to degrees Fahrenheit.

$$T_F = 1.8T_C + 32$$

$$T_F = 1.8(-55°) + 32°$$

$$T_F = -99° + 32°$$

$$T_F = -67°$$

So, -55°C = -67°F

Practice Problem Set 1.6:

Convert each of the following temperatures to the scale indicated.

1. 69°F = _____°C

2. 105°C = _____K

3. 25°C = _____°F

4. 5°F = _____°C

5. -40°F = _____°C

6. 40K = _____°C

7. -12°C = _____°F

8. 660°C = _____°F

9. Liquid nitrogen boils at a temperature of about -196°C. What temperature on the Fahrenheit would this correspond to?

10. If the temperature in a crowded room is about 80°F, then what is the equivalent Celsius temperature?

NOTES

CHAPTER SUMMARY

KEY TERMS TO REMEMBER

percent	proportion
%$^{w/v}$	liter
%$^{v/v}$	meter
%$^{w/w}$	gram
scientific notation	milli-
significant figures	micro-
ratio	nano-

POINTS TO REMEMBER

1. To write a number in scientific notation, put it in the form $a \times 10^n$ where $1 \le a < 10$ and n is an integer.

2. Measurements are approximate numbers and their accuracy and precision are reflected by the decimal places and significant figures in the number. When doing calculations with measured amounts, round the answers according to the rules given in order to give an answer that is as precise as possible without appearing too precise.

3. In a true proportion, cross products will be equal.

4. To make a different volume of a solution having a given ratio of parts, use a proportion to determine the needed amounts.

5. The metric system consists of primary units for the properties of length, mass, and volume together with prefixes that are used with these units to create larger or smaller units. The gram, milligram, microgram, nanogram, liter, and milliliter are some of the units most commonly used in the laboratory.

6. There are several temperature scales in common use in the U. S. These are the Celsius (formerly centigrade), Kelvin and Fahrenheit scales. Since you may need to change scales for some laboratory procedures, be sure that you practice so that you can use the appropriate formula to convert temperatures as needed.

CHAPTER REVIEW PROBLEMS

1. Express the following as percents.

   a. 1/8

   b. 0.025

   c. 0.5 parts in 100 total parts

   d. 3 parts in 15 total parts

   e. 12 parts solute + 18 parts solvent

2. a. If the concentration of a solution is 7 parts to 8 total parts, what would be the concentration of the solution expressed as a percent?

   b. If the concentration of a solution is 0.138, what would be the concentration of the solution expressed as a percent?

3. a. If the concentration of a salt solution is $1.5\%^{W/V}$, how many grams of salt would be present in 100 ml of this solution?

   b. How many grams would be present in 1 liter of this solution?

4. Write each of the following numbers in scientific notation.

   a. 0.0133

   c. 1256.23

   b. 250,000

   d. 0.000000001

NOTES

5. Write each of the following numbers in decimal form.

    a. 3.44×10^{-5} c. 2.561×10^{-9}

    b. 3.44×10^{5} d. 6.0×10^{0}

6. If the number 4.15×10^{19} power is to be written as a whole number, how many zeroes should be added to 415?

7. Determine the correct number of significant digits for each of the following measurements:

    a. 0.01350 mg _____ b. 12350.0 m _____
    c. 1.020 L _____

8. Express each of the following numbers in scientific notation, rounding each off to 3 significant figures.

    a. 0.0060135 _____   c. 23.594 _____
    b. 6,354 _____   d. 0.017000 _____

9. Several objects are weighed on scales of differing sensitivities. The following results were recorded: 2.351 g, 2.50 g, 2.143 g and 2.38 g. Find the average of these weights.

10. Solve the following proportions:

    a. $\dfrac{25}{60} = \dfrac{x}{100}$ _____

    b. $\dfrac{2}{x} = \dfrac{12}{.03}$ _____

11. If there are 2 g of NaCl in 100ml of solution, how many ml of solution of the same concentration would 11 g of NaCl make?

12. How many grams of substance would be required to make 200 ml of solution if 5 g will make 250 ml?

13. Write out the names of the metric system units having the following abbreviations:

   a. mg

   b. μm

   c. cL

14. Fill in the blanks with "smaller than" or "larger than":

   a. 1 microgram is _____ 1 nanogram

   b. 1 liter is _____ 1 milliliter

   c. 1 centiliter is _____ 1 kiloliter

15. Do the following conversions.

   a. 653 mg = _____ng   e. 3.5×10^5 mm = _____m

   b. 0.0025 cm = _____mL   f   1.2 μm = _____cm

   c. 125.3 kg = _____g   g. 6.5 L = _____mL

   d. 350 mL = _____L   h. 0.065 mm = _____nm

16. Do the following calculations expressing all answers with the correct number of significant figures.

   a. 3.55 g + 16 mg + 2534 μg + 5.015 g = _____g

   b. $\dfrac{167 \text{ nm} \times 2.35 \text{ nm}}{2.5 \text{ mm}}$ = _____nm

   c. (4.35×10^{-3})m x (2.00×10^5)m x (6.3×10^{-4})m = _____m^3

17. What is the difference between an exact number and an approximate number?

NOTES

<table>
<tr><td>

NOTES

</td><td>

18. What factors may affect the precision of a measurement taken in a laboratory?

19. Are the measurements 15 g and 15.0 g the same? Why or why not?

20. Which container (A, B or C) contains the most solution?

    A contains 1.36×10^3 nl of solution
    B contains 0.00136 ml of solution
    C contains 1.36 µl of solution

21. 35°C = _____°F

22. 88°F = _____°C

</td></tr>
</table>

SUGGESTED LABORATORY EXERCISES

LABORATORY EXERCISE I: MEASUREMENT ACCURACY

This lab is designed to emphasize the need for attention to accuracy of measurement and the need for care in rounding off when doing mathematical operations with measured quantities.

Equipment required:
➢ Rulers, scales and volumetric containers of varying degrees of precision (all as chosen by your instructor)

Procedures:
A. Measuring the length of this textbook
B. Measuring the weight of a nickel
C. Measuring a quantity of water

Directions:
1. Have each person in your lab group measure the length of their own textbook with a different ruler as supplied by your lab instructor.

2. What is the total length of all the books in your lab group? Remember to round your answer to match the least precise measurement as directed in the rules for rounding measurements when adding.

3. Now remeasure all of the textbooks with the most precise ruler and add them again.

4. Do the totals for steps three and four agree? If not, why not?

NOTES

NOTES

5. Weigh a nickel on several different scales and find the average weight (i.e., add all the various weights and divide by the number of weighings done).

6. Now weigh the nickel on the most precise scale available.

7. Are the weights for steps five and six the same? Why or why not?

8. Next, measure 10 ml of water with several different volumetric measuring instruments such as a graduated cylinder and a pipette.

9. Compare the volume measurements you have made by weighing each on the same scale.

10. Do they agree with each other exactly? Why or why not?

LABORATORY EXERCISE II : SIGNIFICANT FIGURES

Introduction:

In lecture we have discussed how the digits of numbers obtained by common laboratory measurements are determined to be significant. As a direct application of these rules we will generate measured data that we will then manipulate in some simple mathematical procedures. While there are many ways to develop measured data in the lab we will be using the balance to obtain results of numbers with a variety of significant figures.

1. Obtain a penny, nickel, dime and quarter.

2. There are three scales of varying sensitivities available. Weigh your coins separately on each of the 3 scales and record your data below.

3. Find the average weight of the four coins on scale #1, #2, and #3. Are the answers different? Which is the "right" answer?

4. How much does your penny weigh? What is the average weight of your penny, your nickel, your dime and your quarter?

Scale	#1	#2	#3	Average Weight
Weight of penny				
Weight of nickel				
Weight of dime				
Weight of quarter				
Average Weight of 4 Coins				

NOTES

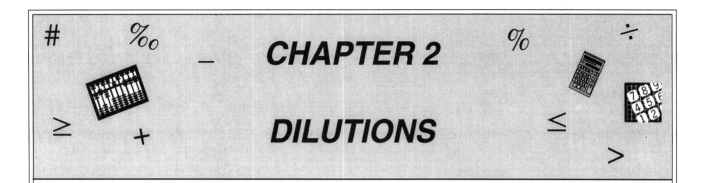

In This Chapter:

The making of a dilution or series of dilutions is a common laboratory procedure. The determination of the correct volumes of solutions needed to perform a dilution and the calculation of the resulting concentration of the dilution or dilution series involve the use of mathematical ratios, proportions and percents. The mathematical calculations related to these procedures are presented and explained in this chapter. It is important that the concepts associated with a dilution procedure as well as the mathematics involved be understood fully.

NOTES

2.1 INTRODUCTION - DILUTION RATIO

One common laboratory procedure requires the addition of one substance to another in order to reduce the concentration of one of the substances. In other words, a weaker solution is made from a stronger solution by adding a diluent such as water to a specific amount of the stronger solution. This process and the resulting mixture is called a **dilution**. In Chapter 1, a ratio was defined in general terms as an amount of one thing relative to another. However, a **dilution ratio**, as used in laboratory procedures, is a very specific ratio. The numerator of the dilution ratio <u>always</u> refers to the number of parts of the substance being diluted. The denominator represents the total number of parts of mixture comprised of the diluent (all diluting agents) and the substance being diluted. Dilution ratios should be reduced to lowest terms and are commonly expressed as the ratio of 1 to a number.

Dilution Ratio = $\dfrac{\text{parts of substance being diluted}}{\text{total number of parts of solution}}$

Example 2.1: Five milliliters of urine are diluted with 15 ml of water. The dilution ratio of this solution is

$$\frac{5 \text{ ml}}{20 \text{ ml total}} \quad \text{or} \quad \frac{1}{4}$$

The denominator is the sum of the amounts of urine and water that comprise the solution.

A dilution ratio is one method of expressing relative concentration. Any volume of a dilution can be made as long as the **relative** parts of the solution remain in the given ratio.

Example 2.2: 1 ml serum + 4 ml diluent = 5 ml total solution resulting in a <u>1</u> dilution ratio.

5

10 ml serum + 40 ml diluent = 50 ml total solution resulting in a $\underline{10}$ or $\underline{1}$ dilution ratio.
    50   5

The dilution ratios are the same even though the volumes of the solutions in the two examples differ.

In general, adding 1 ml of a liquid solute and 4 ml of diluent will produce a 1:5 dilution. However, in some situations, chemical combinations and repositioning of molecules occur when solutions are mixed. This produces slightly different volumes from the expected total. For example, 1 ml of water plus 1 ml of alcohol does not yield 2 ml of solution because of the positioning of molecules that occurs when the two solutions are mixed. A dilution is usually made, therefore, by taking a specific amount of the substance being diluted, placing it in a test tube or beaker, and adding enough diluent to produce the volume needed. This process is called **diluting a substance up to total volume**.

The following symbols should be used when describing a dilution procedure.

COMBINING SPECIFIC VOLUMES OF SUBSTANCES

2 ml serum combined with 10 ml of diluent yields
12 ml of solution

2 ml serum + 10 ml diluent ⇨ 12 ml solution

DILUTING UP TO A SPECIFIED VOLUME

2 ml serum diluted up to 12 ml yields 12 ml of solution

2 ml serum ⇧ 12 ml ⇨ 12 ml solution

Since dilutions are ratios, problems involving dilutions are easily solved using the methods for solving proportions previously discussed. The given dilution ratio is used to set up a proportion that will allow us to calculate the volume of substances needed for a particular dilution.

NOTES

> **NOTES**

Example 2.3: How many milliliters of serum will be needed to make 300 ml of a 1 to 5 dilution of serum in saline?

A $\underline{1}$ dilution means $\underline{\quad 1 \text{ part serum} \quad}$.
  5   5 parts total volume

Let x = amount of serum needed for 300 ml of solution.

Set up the following proportion and solve for x:

$$\frac{x \text{ ml}}{300 \text{ml}} = \frac{1 \text{ part}}{5 \text{ parts}}$$

$$5x = (300)(1) \text{ (cross products)}$$

$$x = 60$$

Therefore, **60 ml** of serum are needed for 300 ml of a $\underline{1}$ dilution
                                                                    5

or in correct notation

60 ml serum ⇧ 300ml ⇨ 300 ml of a $\underline{1}$ dilution.
                                    5

Example 2.4: A sample of 2.5 milliliters of blood needs to be diluted 1 to 50. What will be the final volume of this dilution?

A $\underline{1}$ dilution means $\underline{\quad 1 \text{ part blood} \quad}$.
 50   50 parts total volume

Let x = final volume of this dilution.

$$\frac{1 \text{ part}}{50 \text{ total parts}} = \frac{2.5 \text{ ml}}{x \text{ ml}}$$

$$1x = (50)(2.5) \text{ (cross products)}$$

$$x = 125$$

Therefore, 2.5 ml of blood diluted 1 to 50 will result in a total volume of **125 ml**, or

2.5 ml blood ⇧ 125 ml ⇨ 125 ml of 1/50 dilution.

Example 2.5: You want to make 50 ml of a 1/250 dilution of
urine in water. How much diluent will you need?

First, the amount of urine needed to make 50 ml of a 1/250 dilution
must be calculated.

Let x = amount of urine needed for the dilution.

$$\frac{x \text{ ml}}{50 \text{ ml}} = \frac{1}{250}$$

$$250x = (50)(1) \quad \text{(cross products)}$$

$$\frac{250x}{250} = \frac{50}{250}$$

$$x = 0.2$$

Therefore, 0.2 ml of urine will be needed to make 20 ml of a 1/250
dilution. Since the total volume of the dilution includes urine and
water, the amount of diluent (water) needed can be found by
subtracting the amount of urine in the solution from the total
volume.

Total volume - volume substance = volume diluent
                  being diluted

50 ml   -   0.2 ml   **= 49.8 ml diluent needed**

NOTES

Practice Problem Set 2.1:

Answer each of the following. Reduce all ratios to lowest terms.

1. There are 10 ml of saline in a test tube. Five milliliters of serum are added to the tube. Give the following ratios.

   a. saline to serum
   b. serum to saline
   c. the dilution ratio for the serum

2. If 10 ml of serum are diluted with 35 ml of saline, what is the resulting dilution ratio?

3. The following quantities are placed in a test tube: 0.2 ml of blood; 3.4 ml of water; and 1.4 ml of reagents. What is the dilution ratio of this blood specimen?

4. How much serum is in 75 ml of a 1/5 dilution of serum in saline?

5. How much of a 1/20 dilution will 5 ml of serum make?

6. Determine the amount of serum needed to make 250 ml of a 1/10 dilution.

7. How would you prepare 350 ml of a 2/5 dilution of serum in saline?

8. Three milliliters of urine will make how much of a 1/150 dilution? How much diluent will be needed?

9. If 50 ml of a solution contains 35 ml of diluent, what is the dilution ratio for this solution?

10. If 0.5 ml of concentrated solution is diluted to 10 ml, how much diluent was added to the concentrated solution? What is the resulting dilution ratio?

2.2 CONCENTRATION OF DILUTIONS

When a dilution has been made, the result is a weakened solution. The concentration of the original substance has been changed by the addition of a diluent producing a new solution which is less concentrated than the original. There are many ways of expressing the concentration of a solution. Some of the more common expressions of concentration that we will use include:

1. **Dilution Ratio** - The concentration of a solution may be expressed as a dilution ratio. For example, you could be asked to do a 1/10 dilution of a 1/5 stock solution. The 1/5 ratio, <u>used as an adjective</u>, expresses the concentration of the solution you are to dilute. The 1/10 dilution ratio tells you the "recipe" for mixing this dilution; that is, mix 1 part of the 1/5 stock solution with 9 parts diluent.

2. **Percent -** As presented in Chapter 1, this expression of concentration is defined as parts per 100 parts.

3. **mg/dl** - This is a weight/volume expression of concentration comparing the number of milligrams of solute per 1 deciliter (100 ml) of solution.

4. **Molarity (M)** - This expression of concentration will be discussed more fully in Chapter 3. However, it is also a weight/volume ratio telling the number of moles of solute per 1 liter (1000 ml) of solution.

5. **Normality (N)** - Also discussed more fully in Chapter 3, this concentration unit gives the number of equivalents of solute per 1 liter (1000 ml) of solution. This unit of concentration is commonly used to express the concentrations of acids and bases.

NOTES

Substances such as serum, blood, urine or absolute ethanol are considered to be undiluted. Their concentrations before dilution are expressed as the ratio 1/1. Therefore, if a problem asks you to dilute a substance and no concentration units are given, assume the concentration to be 1/1.

Since a dilution is a new solution which is less concentrated than the original solution, a method of determining the concentration of the new dilution is needed. The new concentration may be calculated with the following formula:

Original Concentration × Dilution Ratio = Concentration of
Resulting Solution

The concentration of the diluted solution should be expressed in the same units as the units of concentration of the original substance. For example, if the original concentration is expressed as a percent, the concentration of the resulting dilution will also be expressed as a percent.

Example 2.6: A 0.5% NaCl solution is diluted 1/10. What is the concentration of the resulting solution?

Original Concentration × Dilution Ratio = New Concentration

$$0.5\% \times \frac{1}{10} = c \qquad \text{(formula)}$$

$$\frac{0.5}{10}\% = c \qquad \text{(multiply)}$$

$$0.05\% = c \qquad \text{(divide to obtain decimal)}$$

Therefore, the concentration of the diluted NaCl solution is **0.05%**.

Example 2.7: A 2 N NaOH solution is diluted 1/25. Give the concentration of the final solution.

Original Concentration × Dilution Ratio = New Concentration

$$2\,N \ \times \ \frac{1}{25} \ = \ c \quad \text{(formula)}$$

$$\frac{2}{25}\,N \ = \ c \quad \text{(multiply)}$$

$$0.08\,N \ = \ c \quad \text{(divide to obtain decimal)}$$

Therefore, the concentration of the diluted NaOH solution is **0.08N**.

Example 2.8: A 1/5 dilution is further diluted by adding 5.5 ml of water to 0.5 ml of the original dilution. What is the concentration of the resulting dilution?

Original concentration of the solution is **1/5**.

Dilution Ratio is 0.5 ml/6.0 ml or **1/12**. (0.5 ml of the original solution mixed with 5.5 ml of H_2O = 6.0 ml total)

Original Concentration × Dilution Ratio = New Concentration

$$1/5 \ \times \ 1/12 \ = \ c$$

$$1/60 \ = \ c$$

Therefore, the concentration of the new dilution is expressed in the same manner as the original, a ratio, **1/60**.

NOTES

NOTES

Practice Problem Set 2.2:

1. A 1/50 dilution of a urine sample is done. What is the concentration of the resulting solution?

2. A 20 N solution is diluted 1/50. What is the resulting concentration?

3. A stock glucose standard has a concentration of 1000 mg/dl. A 1/4 dilution of the standard is done. What is the concentration of the diluted solution?

4. One milliliter of a 1/5 dilution is further diluted by adding 4 ml of diluent to it. What is the concentration of the resulting dilution?

5. A 0.25% solution is diluted 1/100. What is the concentration of the resulting dilution?

6. A 12% solution is diluted 1/10. What is the concentration of the resulting solution? If the new solution is again diluted 1/10, what is the concentration after the second dilution?

7. Describe how to do a 1 to 10 dilution of a 7.5% solution. Give the concentration of the dilution.

8. Ten milliliters of a 2.5 M stock solution are placed in a test tube. This solution is then diluted with 10 ml of water. What is the resulting dilution ratio? What is the new concentration of this dilution?

2.3 INTRODUCTION - DILUTION SERIES

Procedures and testing in a laboratory sometimes require the use of a dilution series. A group of solutions which have different concentrations of the same substance is called a **dilution series**. A dilution series may be an independent series or a dependent series. If a series is done independently, each dilution is separate from all other dilutions done. However, in a dependent series, all subsequent dilutions depend on the preceding dilution.

Several important concepts are associated with dilution series and are described using the following terms.

1. **Final Volume** is the volume in each tube after a dilution series has been completed. If an independent series is done, this will be the volume after each individual dilution is made. If a dependent dilution series is done, some of each dilution will be transferred to make new dilutions, so the final volume in a tube is the amount remaining after the subsequent transfers have been completed.

2. The **Tube Dilution** is the dilution ratio for that particular tube. It is the "recipe" for combining the substance or transfer amount being diluted with the correct amount of diluent in a tube.

3. The **Solution Dilution** is the ratio of the amount of original substance to the total volume prepared in each tube. In an independent series, the solution dilution is the same ratio as the tube dilution. In a dependent series, the solution dilution for any tube can be calculated using the product of all previous tube dilutions done.

4. The **Substance Concentration** is the concentration of the original substance that was diluted in any given tube. It is the product of the beginning concentration of the substance being diluted and the dilutions done to produce the solution in each tube.

2.4 INDEPENDENT DILUTION SERIES

In an **independent dilution**, several different dilutions of a substance are done independently of the other dilutions. The purpose of diluting a substance independently is so that more than one test can be run on the same substance (i.e., white blood count and red blood count from the same blood draw).

Example 2.9: Do the following dilutions of urine in water, making the series independently: 1/10, 1/50, 1/100.

Since no volumes are specified in the problem, the denominators of the tube dilutions are used to indicate what volumes should be made in milliliters.

Tube #1: Mix 1 ml urine with 9 ml water to produce 10 ml total volume.

Tube #2: Mix 1 ml urine with 49 ml water to produce 50 ml total volume.

Tube #3: Mix 1 ml urine with 99 ml water to produce 100 ml total volume.

The **solution dilution** in each tube will be the same ratio as the tube dilution for each tube. Therefore, the solution dilution of Tube #1 is 1/10 meaning that 1/10 of the total volume in the tube is urine and 9/10 is water. Tube #2 is 1/50 urine (solution dilution) and 49/50 water. Tube #3 is 1/100 urine (solution dilution) and 99/100 water.

The calculation of the **concentration** of urine in each tube will be done as follows:

Urine is considered to be "pure" before it is diluted and therefore its concentration will be expressed as the ratio 1/1.

Original Concentration	×	Dilution	=	New Concentration
Tube #1:	1/1	×	1/10 =	1/10
Tube #2:	1/1	×	1/50 =	1/50
Tube #3:	1/1	×	1/100 =	1/100

The new concentration of the solution in each tube is expressed in the same manner as the original, a ratio. Certain types of laboratory equipment, such as a spectrophotometer, require a minimum volume of a solution for accurate testing purposes. If a procedure requires a specific volume in each tube of an independent dilution series, use a proportion to calculate the volumes needed.

Example 2.10: Do a 1/5, 1/10, and 1/50 dilution series of a 1.5 M solution. Do the dilutions independently and produce 25 ml of each dilution.

Tube #1: We need 25 ml of a 1/5 dilution. Use a proportion to calculate the parts needed for this dilution.

$$\frac{1}{5} = \frac{x \text{ ml } 1.5 \text{ M solution}}{25 \text{ ml total volume}}$$

$$5x = 25$$

$$x = 5 \text{ ml of } 1.5 \text{ M solution needed}$$

Tube #2: We need 25 ml of a 1/10 dilution. Use a proportion to calculate the parts needed for this dilution.

$$\frac{1}{10} = \frac{x \text{ ml } 1.5 \text{ M solution}}{25 \text{ ml total volume}}$$

$$10x = 25$$

$$x = 2.5 \text{ ml of } 1.5 \text{ M solution needed}$$

Tube #3: We need 25 ml of a 1/50 dilution. Use a proportion to calculate the parts needed for this dilution.

$$\frac{1}{50} = \frac{x \text{ ml } 1.5 \text{ M solution}}{25 \text{ ml total volume}}$$

$$50x = 25$$

$$x = 0.5 \text{ ml of } 1.5 \text{ M solution needed}$$

Final Dilutions

Tube #1	Tube #2	Tube #3
5 ml 1.5 M sol	2.5 ml 1.5 M sol	0.5 ml 1.5 M sol
+20 ml diluent	+ 22.5 ml diluent	+ 24.5 ml diluent
25 ml total	25.0 ml total	25.0 ml total

$$\frac{5}{25} = \frac{1}{5} \text{ dilution} \qquad \frac{2.5}{25} = \frac{1}{10} \text{ dilution} \qquad \frac{0.5}{25} = \frac{1}{50} \text{ dilution}$$

Again, the **solution dilutions** will be the same as the tube dilutions. Tube #1 has a total volume of 25 ml and 1/5 of that total (5 ml) is 1.5 M solution and 4/5 is diluent. Therefore, the solution dilution of Tube #1 is 1/5.

The **concentrations** of the 1.5 M solution in each tube will be reduced as a result of the dilutions. The concentration of the solutions in the three tubes is caluclated as follows:

Original Concentration × Dilution = New Concentration

Tube #1:	1.5 M	×	1/5	=	0.3 M
Tube #2:	1.5 M	×	1/10	=	0.15 M
Tube #3:	1.5 M	×	1/50	=	0.03 M

The concentrations of the dilutions done are given in the same units as the original solution that was diluted, molarity (M).

Practice Problem Set 2.4:

1. Explain how to do an independent series of dilutions of serum in saline if the tube dilutions are 2/10, 1/20, and 2/25.

2. Fill in the chart below for the independent dilution series described in problem #1.

	Tube #1	Tube #2	Tube #3
Amount of Serum			
Amount of Saline			
Total Volume			
Tube Dilution			
Solution Dilution			
Substance Concentration			

3. If a certain procedure calls for 50 ml final volume for each of the independent dilutions done in problem 1, what volumes of serum and saline would be required for each dilution to produce the required totals? Would these changes in the volumes affect the tube dilutions, solution dilutions and concentrations of the solutions in each tube? Explain your answer.

4. An independent dilution series of a 2 N HCl solution is to be done. The dilution ratios are 1/5, 1/10 and 1/50. Give the concentration of HCl in each of the three tubes after the dilutions are complete.

2.5 DEPENDENT DILUTION SERIES

A more common method of making a dilution series is to make the first dilution and then transfer some of this dilution to another test tube where it is diluted again. Transfers may be repeated as many times as necessary to complete the series. In this type of dilution series all dilutions except the first are **dependent** on previous dilutions. The reduction of concentration is cumulative, lessening with each subsequent dilution. By transferring dilutions, especially in a serial dilution in which reduction is done in equal increments, a controlled decrease of concentration occurs and a quantitative analysis can be done. This type of procedure is useful, for example, when estimates of the volume of antibody in a specimen are needed. The laboratory technician can establish a table of comparisons and plot a standard curve as needed.

Example 2.11: Do a 1/5 dilution of urine in water. Then, redilute it 1/10 and then again 1/20.

This is a dependent dilution series. In the first tube, 1 ml of urine is pipetted into the tube and 4 ml of water is added to it. To make the second dilution, 1 ml of solution from Tube #1 is removed and transferred to Tube #2. Nine milliliters of water is then added to Tube #2 to produce a 1/10 dilution. The third dilution is done by removing 1 ml of solution from Tube #2 and transferring it to Tube #3. Nineteen milliliters of water is added to Tube #3 to produce a 1/20 dilution.

Tubes:	#1	#2	#3
	1 ml urine	1 ml from tube 1	1 ml from tube 2
	+4 ml water	+ 9 ml water	+19 ml water
Volume (before trans)	5 ml total	10 ml total	20 ml total
Volume (after trans)	4 ml	9 ml	20 ml (no transfer)

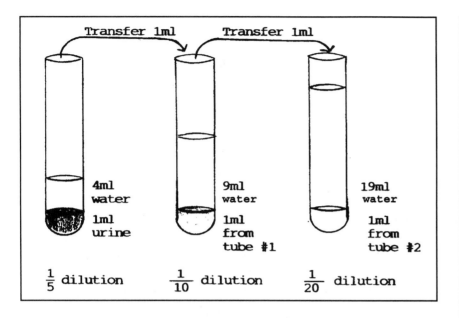

SOLUTION DILUTION

The **solution dilution** in example 2.11 would be calculated by finding the product of all dilutions done to produce the solution in a particular tube in the series. For example, to find the solution dilution of the second tube in a series, multiply the first tube dilution × the second tube dilution.

Solution Dilution = Tube Dilution × Tube Dilution × Tube...
(Dependent Series)

Example 2.11 (cont.): Give the solution dilution in each tube of this dilution series.

The tube dilutions were 1/5, 1/10 and 1/20.

a. The solution dilution of Tube #1 is **1/5**. This means that 1/5 of the solution in Tube #1 is urine and 4/5 is water.

b. The solution dilution of the second Tube is $1/5 \times 1/10 =$ **1/50**. This means that 1/50 of the liquid in tube #2 is urine and 49/50 is water.

c. The solution dilution of Tube #3 is $1/5 \times 1/10 \times 1/20 =$ **1/1000**. This means that 1/1000 of the solution is urine and 999/1000 of the solution is water.

NOTES

NOTES

Remember that the solution dilution is defined to be the ratio of the amount of original substance to the total volume in a tube. As illustrated by the above example, the amount of original substance that is in a solution after several dilutions in a dependent series decreases rapidly as indicated by the rapid decrease in size of the solution dilution ratios.

SUBSTANCE CONCENTRATION

We have already learned that when a concentrated solution is diluted, the concentration of the new solution can be calculated by multiplying the concentration of the solution that was diluted times the dilution ratio. If a series of dilutions is done, we can find the concentration of the solution in any tube by multiplying the original concentration times all dilutions done. Be sure that the final answer is expressed in the same form as the original concentration. If the substance being diluted is pure such as serum, blood, urine or absolute alcohol, the original concentration should be expressed as 1/1.

**Concentration of
    Any Dilution = Original Concentration × Dilutions Done**

Example 2.11 (cont.): Give the concentration of urine in each tube in this dilution series.

First, the concentration of urine is considered to be 1/1.

Original Concentration × Dilutions = New Concentration

Tube #1:   1/1 × 1/5 = 1/5

Tube #2:   1/1 × 1/5 × 1/10 = 1/50

Tube #3:   1/1 × 1/5 × 1/10 × 1/20 = 1/1000

The concentrations of the three tubes are expressed as ratios since the original concentration was a ratio.

Because the substance that was diluted in Example 2.11 was "pure" (no concentration units given), the solution dilutions and concentrations for each tube were the same. If the substance that is diluted has stated concentration units, then the solution dilutions and concentrations will be different.

Example 2.12: A 10% NaCl solution is diluted 1/2 and rediluted 1/5 and again 1/5. What is the solution dilution and concentration of the solution in each tube?

Solution Dilution = Tube Dilution × Tube Dilution × Tube Dilution

Tube #1: Solution Dilution = 1/2

Tube #2: Solution Dilution = 1/2 × 1/5 = 1/10

Tube #3: Solution Dilution = 1/2 × 1/5 × 1/5 = 1/50

Substance Concentration = Original Concentration × Dilutions Done

Tube #1: 10% × 1/2 = 5%

Tube #2: 10% × 1/2 × 1/5 = 1%

Tube #3: 10% × 1/2 × 1/5 × 1/5 = 0.2%

✍ **AN IMPORTANT NOTE:** Formulas are being provided to the student as a guideline for calculations. However, it is essential that the dilution process itself be understood so that the numbers that are derived make sense. No set of formulas can anticipate every problem or procedure that may arise in a laboratory setting. The understanding of the relationships between dilutions, both independent and dependent, and their concentrations is vital to success in this area of study.

NOTES

SERIAL DILUTIONS

Many procedures in a clinical laboratory call for a dilution series of progressive, regular increments in which each subsequent dilution is less concentrated than the preceding one by a constant amount (i.e. all tube dilutions in the series are the same). This type of series is called a **serial dilution**. The term **fold** may be used in describing this type of dilution series. A two-fold series represents a series where every tube dilution is 1/2; a five-fold is 1/5; and a ten-fold is 1/10. In some situations, the first dilution of a series may use one tube dilution and subsequent dilutions are done with different but consistent tube dilutions. For example, the first dilution may be a 1/10 dilution followed by three five-fold (1/5) dilutions.

Example 2.13: You are given a series of 5 tubes, each containing 6.0 ml of saline. One ml of serum is added to the first tube and then a serial dilution using 1.5 ml is carried out. Give the tube dilution for each of the 5 tubes.

Tubes:	#1	#2	#3
	1.0 ml serum	1.5 ml from #1	1.5 ml from #2
	+ 6.0 ml saline	+ 6.0 ml saline	+ 6.0 ml saline
	7.0 ml total	7.5 ml total	7.5 ml total

Tube Dilution:	$\dfrac{1}{7}$	$\dfrac{1.5}{7.5} = \dfrac{1}{5}$	$\dfrac{1.5}{7.5} = \dfrac{1}{5}$

Tubes:	#4	#5
	1.5 ml from #3	1.5 ml from #4
	+6.0 ml saline	+6.0 ml saline
	7.5 ml total	7.5 ml total

Tube Dilution:	$\dfrac{1.5}{7.5} = \dfrac{1}{5}$	$\dfrac{1.5}{7.5} = \dfrac{1}{5}$

The first dilution was 1/7 followed by a five-fold serial dilution.

The dilution fold of a serial dilution can be determined using the following formula:

$$\frac{\text{volume transferred}}{\text{total volume}} = \frac{1}{\text{dilution fold}}$$

As in the above example, if 1.5 ml of solution is transferred serially from one tube to the next and each time is added to 6.0 ml of diluent, the fold would be 1.5/7.5 or **1/5** indicating a **five-fold** serial dilution.

NOTES

NOTES

Practice Problem Set 2.5:

1. Explain how to do a dependent series of dilutions of serum in saline if the tube dilutions are 1/10, 1/25, and 1/50. What would be the solution dilution for each tube?

2. A dependent dilution series of urine in water is done. The solution dilution of the 4th tube in the series is 1/250. There is 100 ml of solution in the tube. How much of the total is urine and how much is water?

3. A ten-fold dilution series is done. What is the tube dilution of the third tube in the series? What is the solution dilution for the third tube?.

4. A series of five two-fold dilutions of concentrated solution is to be done. Four milliliters of diluent is put into each tube. How much concentrated solution will be put into Tube #1? Explain the steps needed to complete the series of 5 dilutions.

5. Complete the following chart of values for a dependent dilution series of serum in saline diluted 1/10, rediluted 2/50 and again 4/25.

	Tube #1	Tube #2	Tube #3
Amt. of Solution to be Diluted			
Amount of Diluent			
Total Volume			
Final Volume (after transfer)			
Tube Dilution			
Solution Dilution			

6. A five-fold dilution of serum in saline is performed. If 3 dilutions are done,
   a. What is the tube dilution of each tube?
   b. What is the solution dilution of each tube?
   c. Give the concentration of serum in each tube.

7. A 5% NaCl solution is diluted 1/5 and then rediluted 1/10. What is the final solution dilution? What is the concentration of the solution in the last tube?

8. A 1/5 dilution is diluted 1/10 and again 1/10. What is the final solution dilution? What is the final concentration?

9. Complete the chart below with the correct values for a two-fold dilution series of a 2.5 M solution. Each tube will contain 4 ml of diluent. Calculate the necessary volumes and ratios for this dilution series.

	Tube #1	Tube #2	Tube #3
Amt. of Solution to be Diluted			
Amount of Diluent	4 ml	4 ml	4 ml
Total Volume			
Final Volume (after transfer)			
Tube Dilution			
Solution Dilution			
Substance Concentration			

NOTES

2.6 DILUTION CORRECTION FACTORS

Some solutions are too strong to be tested as they are. Therefore before a test is performed, the sample must be diluted. For example, in performing a test on a urine sample, if the concentration of the substance to be tested for is too high to be determined with a certain procedure, a dilution will be necessary. When giving a test result based on a diluted solution, the results obtained must be corrected mathematically to compensate for the dilution done. To do this, we use a **dilution correction factor** which is defined to be the reciprocal of any dilution ratio that was used to dilute a sample before testing. This factor is multiplied by the results obtained when the diluted substance was tested to give an accurate report for the undiluted sample.

**Reported
Results = Results Obtained × Dilution Correction Factor**

Example 2.13: A blood sample is diluted 1/500; 450 cells are counted in the diluted sample. What result should be reported for the undiluted sample?

Since the blood sample was diluted 1/500, the original undiluted sample contains 500 times as many cells as the diluted sample. The dilution correction factor is 500, so

450 cells in dilution × 500 = 225,000 cells in undiluted sample.

Practice Problem Set 2.6:

1. The result of a bilirubin determination was 2.3 mg/dl. The original specimen had been diluted 1/10. What report should be given for the undiluted specimen?

2. If the results of a glucose determination were 60 mg/dl and the original specimen had been diluted 1/5 and again 1/5, what results should be reported for the original specimen?

NOTES

NOTES

CHAPTER SUMMARY

KEY TERMS TO REMEMBER

Dilution Ratio   Tube Dilution
Dilution Series   Solution Dilution
Independent Series   Substance Concentration
Dependent Series   Dilution Correction Factor
Two-Fold Series   Five-Fold Series
Ten-Fold Series

FORMULAS TO REMEMBER

$$\text{Dilution Ratio} = \frac{\text{parts of substance being diluted}}{\text{total number of parts of solution}}$$

Solution Dilution = tube dilution × tube dilution × ...
(dependent dilution series)

Concentration of
Final Solution   =   original concentration × dilution ratios

Reported Results =   original results × dilution correction
factor

$$\text{Serial Dilution Fold} \quad \frac{1}{\text{dilution fold}} = \frac{\text{volume transferred}}{\text{total volume}}$$

CHAPTER REVIEW PROBLEMS

1. If 50 ml of saline is added to 6 ml of serum, what is the

   a. dilution ratio of the serum

   b. serum to saline ratio

2. A stock glucose standard has a concentration of 100 mg/dl. A 1/50 dilution of the standard is done. What is the concentration of the resulting dilution?

3. How much of a 1/50 dilution can be made with 4 ml of urine?

4. A 0.5% solution is diluted 1/50 and rediluted 1/10. What is the concentration of the resulting dilution?

5. If you were asked to dilute a serum sample 2/10, redilute 4/25 and again 4/50, and you made them as stated,

   a. Describe the procedure that you would follow.

   b. What volume would you have of each dilution remaining in the three test tubes when the dilution series was completed?

6. A 1/10 dilution is diluted 3/10 and again 1/100. What is the final solution dilution? What is the concentration of the final solution in the series?

NOTES

7. A 15% solution is to be diluted with water using a series of four dilutions. The dilution in Tube #1 is to be 1/5 followed by a two-fold dilution series.

    a. What would be the concentration of the solution in the third tube?

    b. If the procedure calls for using 3 ml of original solution for the first dilution, what amount of diluent would be needed to produce the desired 1/5 dilution ratio in the first tube?

    c. What is the solution dilution in the fourth tube? This fraction indicates the fractional amount of original solution in this tube. What fractional part of the solution in the fourth tube is water?

8. You are asked to dilute a 6 N NaOH solution 2/5, redilute 1/10, and again 2/50. Produce 50 ml of solution in each tube before transfer. Fill in the missing numbers in the chart.

	Tube #1	Tube #2	Tube #3
Amt. of Solution to be Diluted			
Amount of Diluent			
Total Volume	50 ml	50 ml	50 ml
Final Volume (after transfer)			
Tube Dilution			
Solution Dilution			
Substance Concentration			

9. How would you prepare 250 ml of a 2/5 dilution of alcohol in water? What would the concentration of this dilution be?

10. If 150 ml of a solution of serum in saline contain 90 ml of saline, what is the dilution ratio for this solution?

11. A urine specimen is diluted 2/50 and then rediluted 1/10 for testing purposes. The results of the test for the diluted specimen are 50 mg/dl. What should be reported as results for the undiluted specimen?

12. What is the resulting concentration of a solution if 25 ml of a 4.5 N is diluted up to 100 ml?

13. A 1/5 dilution of a 5% solution is done. In a second tube, a 5/25 dilution of the same solution is done. Is the amount of 5% solution in each tube different? Is the concentration of 5% solution in each tube different? Why or why not?

14. A white blood count is done on a blood sample that has been diluted 1/20. The number of cells counted in the sample is 2022 cells/mm^3. What number should be reported for the undiluted sample?

NOTES

NOTES

SUGGESTED LABORATORY EXERCISES

LABORATORY EXERCISE 1: DEMONSTRATION OF A DEPENDENT SERIAL DILUTION

A simple lab exercise to illustrate the idea of a dilution series can be done by using colored water and tap water to dilute if chemicals and instruments are not readily available to the class. Taking colored water and doing a 1/2, 1/5 or 1/10 serial dilution will give students a visual picture of the process they have been discussing in this chapter.

LABORATORY EXERCISE 2: QUANTITATIVE ANALYSIS USING A SERIAL DILUTION

This lab will illustrate the process of doing a serial dilution and obtaining absorbance readings from a spectrophotometer which will then be related to concentrations using Beer's Law.

Equipment required:
➢ 1.0 M standard solution of cobalt chloride hexahydrate
➢ de-ionized water for the diluent
➢ pipettes, bulbs, test tubes, test tube racks
➢ spectrophotometer and cuvets for use in the spec 20

Procedures:

1. You are trying to determine the unknown concentration of a sample solution containing cobalt chloride hexahydrate. An appropriate approach is to prepare a serial dilution with 5 different concentrations using a 2- or 5- fold serial dilution series. Do the serial dilution using the chart below to help you organize your figures. Then measure the absorbance readings for each of your dilutions using the spectrophotometer as demonstrated by your lab instructor. A minimum volume of 4 ml will be needed after transfer for accurate reading on the spectrophotometer. Use a wavelength of 510 nm and a blank with de-ionized water for calibration of the machine. Record these readings in the chart provided on the next page. Then find the absorbance reading for the sample whose concentration you are trying to calculate.

2. The relationship of absorbance to concentration is expressed in the equation known as Beer's Law.

$$A = abC \quad \text{where} \quad \begin{aligned} A &= \text{absorbance} \\ C &= \text{concentration of colored solution} \\ a &= \text{absorptiviy coefficient (constant)} \\ b &= \text{length of light path through the cuvet (constant)} \end{aligned}$$

Since a and b are constants, A is directly proportional to C. Therefore, if solutions of known concentration are measured in the spectrophotometer and absorbance readings obtained, the concentrations of unknown samples can be calculated using this proportion: $\dfrac{A_u}{C_u} = \dfrac{A_s}{C_s}$ or $C_u = A_u \times \dfrac{C_s}{A_s}$

Use this proportion to calculate the concentration of the unknown sample whose absorbance reading you obtained from the spectrophotometer. Use any of the readings from the dilution series as the absorbance and concentration of the standard (A_s, C_s). This procedure could be done for any number of unknown samples. The determination of concentration for unknown samples can also be done by using the absorbance readings and their matching concentrations to plot a standard curve. This method will be discussed in detail in a later chapter.

NOTES

		NOTES			

CHART OF VALUES FOR A 1/2 OR 1/5 SERIAL DILUTION

	Tube #1	Tube #2	Tube #3	Tube #4	Tube #5
Volume to be diluted (ml)					
Volume Diluent					
Total Volume					
Volume after transfer (min. 4 ml)					
Tube Dilution					
Solution Dilution					
Substance Concentration					
Absorbance readings					

The absorbance reading for the unknown sample is:_____.

In This Chapter:

The performance of accurate and precise chemical analyses is important in a laboratory. Many reagents or solutions that are used for testing purposes are available in prepackaged kits. However, certain reagents or solutions must be prepared from chemicals of recommended purity. Therefore, the student needs to be familiar with the calculations needed to determine volumes and concentrations of solutions or mixtures of solutions. This chapter will discuss the preparation of solutions using various types of concentration units.

NOTES

3.1 INTRODUCTION - SOLUTIONS

A **solution** can be defined as a mixture of two or more substances. Although chemical reactions can occur in solutions, the substances in a solution are not in chemical combination with each other. The substance that is dissolved to make the solution is called the **solute** and the substance that dissolves it is known as the **solvent**. A solution may be either gaseous, liquid or solid. This chapter will focus on the preparation of liquid solutions.

In working with solutions, it is important to know or to be able to measure the concentration of substances in a solution. **Concentration** is defined to be the amount of one substance in a solution relative to the amounts of the other substances in a solution. Concentration values are given as relative measurements such as grams per liter (g/L) or milligrams per deciliter (mg/dl).

The relative units for a solution may be implied by the concentration units that are used for expressing the concentration of a particular solution. Some of the more common expressions of concentration used in the laboratory are listed below with a brief definition of each.

PARTS - The use of this term gives the relationships of substances in a solution without specifying particular units of measure. For example, mix 1 part A with 2 parts B could mean to mix 1 ml A with 2 ml B or 10 g A with 20 g B.

PERCENT - Percent means per 100. As a concentration, percent is defined to be parts of solute per 100 parts of solution. Percent may be used to express weight per unit weight, weight per unit volume, or volume per unit volume.

MOLARITY - Molarity is a concentration unit that expresses the number of moles of solute in 1 liter of solution. This unit of concentration is used to express weight per unit volume. The gram molecular weight of a mole of solute is calculated to be the grams of a substance equal to its atomic or molecular weight.

NORMALITY - Normality is a concentration unit that expresses the number of equivalents of solute in 1 liter of solution. Like molarity, this expression of concentration is a weight per unit volume measurement. An equivalent weight is the amount of an element or compound that will combine with or replace one mole of hydrogen in a chemical reaction. This unit of concentration is commonly used for expressing the concentration of acids or bases.

SPECIFIC GRAVITY - Specific gravity is a method of measuring **density**, the amount of matter per unit volume of substance. When given the required number of grams of pure solute needed to make a solution, specific gravity allows the technician to calculate the volume of a concentrated commercial liquid that is needed to produce the prescribed solution.

NOTES

NOTES

3.2 PREPARATION OF SOLUTIONS USING PARTS

Occasionally, the directions for making a particular solution will be given using parts to be combined. Though not highly recommended for the preparation of solutions because of its non-specific units, this method of expressing concentration is still widely used. For example, a paint store recommends the preparation of a solution of chlorine bleach and water for washing the mildew off of a house. The directions are to mix 1 part chlorine bleach with 3 parts water. These general units allow you to mix 1 ounce of bleach with 3 ounces of water or 1 liter of bleach with 3 liters of water depending on the volumes needed for the job.

When doing a procedure using parts, the same units of measure should be used throughout. The use of parts is implied whenever a unitless ratio is stated such as one-to-one or fifty-to-one. Using a proportion in these problems enables you to easily calculate the specific volumes needed to make the desired solution.

Example 3.1: The labeled instructions on a can of herbicide call for mixing 1 part chemical to 16 parts water. How much of the concentrated chemical should be mixed with 1 gallon of water?

We will measure our chemical in ounces so we must first convert gallons to ounces so that our units are consistent.

There are 128 ounces in 1 gallon.

$$\frac{1 \text{ part chemical}}{16 \text{ parts water}} = \frac{x \text{ oz. chemical}}{128 \text{ oz. water}}$$

$$16x = 128$$

$$x = 8 \text{ ounces chemical}$$

Therefore, mix 8 ounces of concentrated chemical with 128 ounces (1 gallon) of water to make a solution with the correct strength or concentration.

3.3 PREPARATION OF SOLUTIONS USING % CONCENTRATION

When a concentration is given as a percent, it can be expressed as the ratio of the number of parts of solute to 100 parts of total solution. As defined in Chapter 1, percents can be expressions of weight per unit volume, volume per unit volume, or weight per unit weight. Look at the following percents expressed as ratios of parts.

$$5\%^{w/v} = \frac{5 \text{ g}}{100 \text{ ml}} \qquad 5\%^{v/v} = \frac{5 \text{ ml}}{100 \text{ ml}} \qquad 5\%^{w/w} = \frac{5 \text{ g}}{100 \text{ g}}$$

These ratios can be used to calculate the parts needed to make a particular volume of solution whose concentration is stated as a %. It is important to note that the denominator in these ratios represents the total volume or total weight of the final solution so that $5\%^{w/v}$ means 5 g solute in 100 ml total solution. If extreme precision is needed in the preparation of a solution, the use of the weight/weight ratio for concentration should be used since mass does not vary with temperature as volume does. Though not as convenient, the mass of liquids can be obtained and used to make solutions. Remember that a solute is **diluted up to** (⇧) a total volume when preparing a solution with a weight/volume or volume/volume ratio. However, when preparing a solution using a weight/weight ratio, the masses of the solute and solvent are represented as a sum.

Example 3.2: How much $10\%^{w/v}$ NaCl solution can be made using 30 grams of NaCl?

By definition, $10\%^{w/v} = \dfrac{10\ g}{100\ ml}$

Using a proportion, $\dfrac{10\ g}{100\ ml} = \dfrac{30\ g}{x\ ml}$

$10x = 3000$
(cross products)

$x = 300\ ml$

Therefore, 30 g of NaCl will make 300 ml of a $10\%^{w/v}$ NaCl solution.

Example 3.3: How many grams of NaCl will be needed to make 500 ml of a $15\%^{w/w}$ NaCl solution?

By definition, $15\%^{w/w} = \dfrac{15\ g}{100\ g}$

Using a proportion, $\dfrac{15\ g}{100\ g} = \dfrac{x\ g}{500\ g}$

$100x = 7500$ (cross products)

$x = 75\ g$

Therefore, 75 g of NaCl + 425 g H_2O are needed to produce 500 g of a $15\%^{w/w}$ NaCl solution.

If the parts that comprise the solution are known, the percent (%) concentration can be easily calculated. The following example gives two methods for determining the percent concentration. (These methods were explained in more detail in Chapter 1.) Either method will produce the correct answer. Use the one that makes sense to you.

Example 3.4: A solution contains 15 ml of alcohol in 250 ml of solution. What is the percent concentration of the alcohol?

METHOD A: Change to % using ratio/proportion

$$x\%^{v/v} = \frac{x\ ml}{100\ ml} = \frac{15\ ml}{250\ ml}$$

$$250x = 1500$$

$$x = 6$$

Therefore, the concentration of the solution is

$$\frac{6\ ml}{100\ ml} = 6\%^{v/v}.$$

METHOD B: Change fraction to a decimal and then to %.

$$\frac{15\ ml}{250\ ml} = (15 \div 250) \times 100 = \%$$

$$(.06) \times 100 = \%$$

$$6 = \%$$

Therefore, the concentration of the solution is $6\%^{v/v}$.

NOTES

Practice Problem Set 3.3:

1. The directions on a box of pesticide read: "Mix 1 part bug killer to 5 parts water." How much of the concentrated bug killer should be mixed with 1.5 liters of water?

2. Convert $15\%^{w/v}$ to grams per liter, and then to milligrams per liter.

3. You have 8 g of solute. It take 2 g to make 20 ml of solution. The 8 g will make ____ ml of solution and its percent concentration will be _____.

4. How many grams of salt would be required to make the following?

   a. 100 ml of a 15% solution

   b. 500 ml of a 5% solution

   c. 75 ml of a 4% solution

5. How would you make 1500 g of a $6.5\%^{w/w}$ saline solution?

6. Twenty grams of NaOH are contained in 500 ml of a solution. What is the percent concentration of this solution?

7. A procedure calls for a mixture of 1 part liquid soap to 10 parts water, v/v. If you have 175 ml of water, how much soap will be needed for this mixture?

8. You have 50 ml of a $2.5\%^{w/v}$ NaOH solution. How much NaOH is present in those 50 ml?

9. Explain how to prepare 100 ml of:

   a. a $4.5\%^{w/v}$ NaCl solution
   b. a $4.5\%^{w/w}$ NaCl solution

10. You have 3 g of sucrose ($C_{12}H_{22}O_{11}$). You need to make a $1.5\%^{w/v}$ sucrose solution. How much solution will be produced using the 3 g?

11. Give the percent concentration of the following solutions:

   a. 12 g NaCl ⇧ 150 ml

   b. 1300 mg HCl ⇧ 50 ml

   c. 1.6 ml of HNO_3 ⇧ 0.1 L

   d. 1300 mg of HCl + 90 g H_2O

12. How many grams of sodium chloride are there in 2.5 L of a 0.4% solution?

13. A 2.5%$^{w/v}$ solution can be made by diluting _____ of solute to a total volume of 1 liter. Only _____ of solute will be needed to produce 500 ml of a 2.5%$^{w/v}$ solution.

14. If 5 g of salt is added to 35 g H_2O, what is the concentration (in %) of the resulting solution.

15. How much 25%$^{v/v}$ alcohol solution can be produced with 175 ml of ethyl alcohol?

NOTES

NOTES

3.4 CONCENTRATIONS IN MOLARITY

A **mole** is a unit of measurement for an extremely great number of items. Its value is 6.022×10^{23} which is called Avagadro's number (in honor of Amedeo Avagadro, an Italian physicist). It is one of the seven base units in the International System and is the unit used to denote an amount of substance. A mole is a counting unit in much the same way as a dozen. It is possible to have both a dozen pencils and a mole of pencils. Of course, a mole of pencils is an astronomically large number of pencils.

Another way of defining a mole is as an amount of a substance containing the same number of formula units as there are atoms in exactly 12 g of carbon-12. In other words, 1 mole of carbon = 6.022×10^{23} atoms of carbon which have an atomic mass in grams of 12 g. A formula unit is the atom or molecule indicated by the formula of the substance being used. From these definitions, we can say that the atomic mass in grams of any element contains one mole of atoms.

Mass of 1 Mole = Weight of 6.022×10^{23} Atoms = Atomic Mass

The molar mass of an element is its atomic mass in grams (which contains 1 mole of atoms of that element). To determine the molar mass of an element, change the units of the atomic mass found in the periodic table from amu to grams. Hence, one mole of Fe (that is, 6.022×10^{23} atoms of Fe) would have a molar mass of 55.85 g.

Molarity is a numerical expression of concentration that indicates the number of moles of solute in one liter of solution (mol/L). A saline solution that has a concentration 3 M contains 3 moles of salt per liter of solution. The weight of the salt in the solution is calculated by finding the gram molecular weight of 1 mole and multiplying it by the number of moles. Since the gram molecular weight of salt is 58.5 g, a liter of solution that has a concentration of 3 M contains 3×58.5 g or 175.5 g of salt.

Molarity = Moles of Solute per Liter of Solution = mol/L

If a solution having a concentration expressed in molarity is to be prepared, calculations must be done to determine how many grams of solute should be used to prepare the solution. The amount needed will depend on the gram molecular weight of the solute, the volume of solution needed and the strength of solution to be prepared.

The following formula can be used to calculate the grams of a substance needed to make a solution of any volume having a specific molar concentration. Be sure to note that the volume unit in the formula is liters since molarity indicates moles per liter. Therefore, conversions from milliliter to liters before using the formula may be necessary in many problems.

Molecular × Molarity × Volume Desired = Grams in
Weight   in Liters   Solution

Example 3.5: Make 500 ml of a 0.5 M saline solution.

NaCl has a gram molecular weight of 58.5 g.

Formula: Molecular × Molarity × Volume = Grams in
Weight   in Liters   Solution

$$58.5 \frac{g}{mol} \times 0.5 \frac{mol}{} \times 0.5 \cancel{L} = 14.625 \text{ grams needed}$$

Therefore, to make a 0.5 M saline solution:

14.625 g NaCl ⇧ 500 ml ⇨ 500 ml of 0.5 M saline solution

The above formula can also be used to find any one of the variables if you are given the other three figures to work with. For example, if you know the volume of a particular solution, the type

NOTES

NOTES

of solute used and the grams of solute in the solution, this formula can be used to calculate the molarity of the solution. However, if we solve this formula for molarity, we can derive a direct formula for calculating the molarity of a solution as follows:

$$M = \frac{Grams/Liter}{Molecular\ Weight}$$

This formula allows direct calculation of the concentration in molarity if the type of solute, grams of solute in the solution, and volume of the solution are given. Look at the following example.

Example 3.6: There are 150g of salt in 500 ml of a saline solution. What is the molarity of the solution?

NaCl has a gram molecular weight of 58.5 g.

Formula: $M = \frac{Grams/Liter}{Molecular\ Weight}$

$$M = \frac{150\ g/0.5L}{58.5\ g/mol}$$

$$M = \frac{300\ g/L}{58.5\ g/mol}$$

$$M = 5.1282\ mol/L$$

Therefore, the concentration of this solution is 5.13 M.

A **millimole** (mmol) is 1/1000 of a mole and is expressed as milligram molecular weight. A solution that is 1 M contains 1 mole/liter of solute or 1000 mmol/liter of solute. This fraction can also be expressed as 1000 mmol/1000 ml or 1 mmol/ml. Therefore, the following relationships exist:

Definition Formula

M = Moles/Liter or Millimoles/Milliliter

If a solution is 3.5 M, then it contains 3.5 moles of solute in one liter of solution or 3.5 millimoles of solute in one milliliter of solution. If the molecular weight of the solute is 40, then the solution contains 3.5×40 or 140 g/liter or 140 mg/ml.

Example 3.7:   There are 100 mmol NaOH/400 ml. What is the molarity of the solution?

$$M \; = \; \frac{\text{millimoles}}{\text{milliliter}} \; = \; \frac{100 \text{ mmol}}{400 \text{ ml}} \; = \; 0.25 \text{ M}$$

Therefore, the solution has a concentration 0.25 M.

NOTES

Practice Problem Set 3.4:

1. If you had 5 mol in 500 ml of solution, what would be the molarity of this solution?

2. How many millimoles would be in a liter of solution labeled 1.5 M?

3. What is the gram molecular weight of:
   a. HCl
   b. H_2SO_4
   c. NaOH
   d. $CaCl_2$

4. What weight of NaOH would be required to prepare 2500 ml of a 2.5 M solution?

5. How many grams of H_2SO_4 does 600 ml of a 1.2 M H_2SO_4 solution contain?

6. What weight of HCl is required to prepare 300 ml of a 0.7 M solution?

7. How much 2.5 M solution will 150 g of $CuSO_4$ make?

8. There are 150 g of $CaCl_2$ per 300 ml of solution. What is the molarity of this solution?

9. Describe how to make a 1 M solution of Na_2SO_4.

10. How many nanograms of NaCl would 500 ml of a 1×10^{-8} M solution contain?

11. There are 20 mmol HCl/50 ml. What is the molarity of the solution?

12. A solution contains 4.8 g of $CaCl_2$ in 1 L. How many millimoles does it contain?

13. How many grams of NaCl would be needed to prepare the following solutions:

   a. 1 L of a 3 M solution

   b. 500 ml of a 2 M solution

   c. 1500 ml of a 4.5 M solution

   d. 50 ml of a 0.4 M solution

14. Six grams of NaOH are used to make a 2 M solution. What is the volume in milliliters of the resulting solution?

15. Explain the steps necessary to prepare 500 ml of a 1.5 M $NaHCO_3$ solution.

NOTES

3.5 CONCENTRATIONS IN NORMALITY

Normality is a concentration unit which is based on a unit of mass called the **equivalent weight**, rather than the gram molecular weight used for molarity. The normality of a solution is the concentration expressed as the number of **equivalents** of solute in one liter of solution (eq/L). The weight of an equivalent (called equivalent weight) of a substance is the mass of that substance that will combine with or replace 1 mole of hydrogen.

Normality = Equivalents of Solute per Liter of Solution = eq/L

One application of normality and equivalents is in acid-base neutralization reactions. An equivalent of an acid is that mass of the acid that will furnish 1 mol of H^+ ions. An equivalent of a base is that mass of base that will furnish 1 mol of OH^- ions. Using concentrations in normality, 1 equivalent of acid will react with one equivalent of base.

Sodium hydroxide (NaOH) dissociates completely into one Na^+ ion and one OH^- ion. Hydrochloric acid (HCl) dissociates completely into one H^+ ion and one Cl^- ion. The reaction of 1 mole of HCl + 1 mole of NaOH produces NaCl + H_2O. However, if H_2SO_4 (sulfuric acid) is combined with NaOH, it will require 2 moles of NaOH to neutralize 1 mole of H_2SO_4 or 1 mole NaOH + 0.5 mole H_2SO_4 will result in a neutral solution. Therefore, the equivalent weights needed for this neutralization to occur would be: 1 mole × 40 g (mol. wt.) = 40 g of NaOH and 0.5 mole × 98 g (mol. wt.) = 49 g of H_2SO_4.

A 1 normal (N) solution contains 1 equivalent of solute in 1 liter (1000 ml) of solution. As a general rule, the equivalent weight of an element or compound is equal to the molecular weight divided by the positive valence of the compound. In a monovalent compound (valence +1) such as HCl, molecular weight = equivalent weight. However, compounds with valences greater than 1 such as H_2SO_4 (valence +2) will have equivalent weights less than molecular weights (equivalent weight = 98 g/2 = 49 g).

$$Equivalent\ Weight\ =\ \frac{Molecular\ Weight}{Positive\ Valence}$$

The procedure for calculating grams needed to make a solution whose concentration is expressed using normality is very similar to the procedure for molarity. The only difference in the formulas is the use of equivalent weight for the normality formula in place of the molecular weight that was used for molarity calculations.

$$\begin{matrix} Equivalent & \times & Normality & \times & Volume\ in & = & Grams\ in \\ Weight & & & & Liters & & Solution \end{matrix}$$

Example 3.8: Make 1500 ml of a 2 N HCl solution.

Molecular weight of HCl = 36.5 g

Equivalent weight of HCl = $36.5 \div 1$ = 36.5 g

Equivalent Weight × Normality × Volume in Liters = Grams in Solution

$$(36.5\ \underline{g})\ (2\ \frac{eq}{eq})\ (1.5\ \cancel{L})\ =\ x\ grams$$

$$109.5\ g\ =\ x$$

Therefore, 109.5 g of HCl are needed to make 1500 ml of a 2 N solution.

or

109.5 g HCl ⇧ 1500 ml ⇨ 1500 ml of 2 N HCl solution

If the grams of solute, type of solute and volume of solution are all given, the normality of a solution can be calculated using the above formula or this derivation of that formula:

$$\text{Normality} = \frac{\text{Grams/Liter}}{\text{Equivalent Weight}}$$

Example 3.9: What is the normality of a H_3PO_4 solution that contains 15 g of H_3PO_4 in 500 ml of solution?

Molecular weight of $H_3PO_4 = 98$ g

Equivalent weight of $H_3PO_4 = 98 \div 3 = 32.67$ g

$$\text{Normality} = \frac{\text{grams/liter}}{\text{equivalent weight}}$$

$$N = \frac{15 \text{ g/.5 L}}{32.67 \text{ g/eq}}$$

$$N = \frac{30 \text{ g/L}}{32.67 \text{ g/eq}}$$

$$N = 0.92 \text{ eq/L or } 0.92 \text{ N}$$

Therefore, the concentration of this solution is 0.92 N.

A milliequivalent (mEq) is 1/1000 of an equivalent. The equivalent weight expressed in milligrams will equal 1 mEq. A 1 N solution contains 1 eq/L or 1000 mEq/L. This fraction can also be expressed as 1000 mEq/1000 ml or, by reducing this fraction, 1 mEq/ml. The definition of normality can be expanded in terms of milliequivalents as follows:

Definition Formula

$$\text{Normality} = \frac{\text{Equivalents}}{\text{Liter}} = \frac{\text{Milliequivalents}}{\text{Milliliters}}$$

Example 3.10: How many milliequivalents are in 500 ml of a 2.5 N acid solution?

By definition: 2.5 N = 2.5 mEq/ml

To calculate the number of milliequivalents in 500 ml use a proportion:

$$\frac{2.5 \text{ mEq}}{1 \text{ ml}} = \frac{x \text{ mEq}}{500 \text{ ml}}$$

$$x = 1250 \text{ mEq}$$

Therefore, there are 1250 mEq in 500 ml of a 2.5 N solution.

Practice Problem Set 3.5:

1. How many equivalents of solute are contained in:
    a. 1 L of 4 N solution   c. 500 ml of 8 N
    b. 2 L of 2 N solution

2. How many equivalents of NaOH are there in 4 L of 0.6 N NaOH? in 4 L of 0.6 N HCl?

3. What would be the normality of 38 g of NaOH in 500 ml of solution?

4   What is the equivalent weight of:

    a. HCl   c. NaOH

    b. H_2SO_4 d. $CaCl_2$

5. How many milliliters of a 3 N solution can be made from 50 g of $CaCl_2$?

6. How many grams of solute does 1 L of a 2.5 N Na_2CO_3 solution contain?

7. There are 20 mEq HCl/500 ml. What is the normality?

8. Explain how to prepare 400 ml of 0.05 N $BaSO_4$.

9. How many milliequivalents are in 1 L of a 0.4 N HCl solution?

10. What is the normality of 500 ml of solution containing 25 g of H_3PO_4?

11. How many grams of K_3PO_4 would be needed to prepare the following solutions:

    a. 1 L of 3 N solution

    b. 500 ml of 2 N solution

    c. 1500 ml of 4.5 N solution

    d. 50 ml of 0.4 N solution

12. Ten grams of HCl are used to make a 0.5 N solution. What is the volume in milliliters of the resulting solution?

13. How many grams of solute does 1.5 L of a 0.6 N $Ba(OH)_2$ solution contain?

NOTES

NOTES

3.6 USING SPECIFIC GRAVITY

Specific gravity is a method of measuring **density**, or the amount of matter in a specific volume. When working with concentrated commercial liquids, it is awkward to measure volume in grams. Converting grams to milliliters can be done using specific gravity and thereby making the preparation of the solution easier.

Specific gravity is a ratio of mass to volume. It is defined to be a ratio between the mass of a substance and the mass of an equal volume of pure water at 4° C. It can be expressed as g/ml or ml/g because 1 milliliter of water has a mass of 1 gram. When a bottle label gives the specific gravity of that solution, that number indicates the mass of 1 ml of that solution. For example, a bottle containing a solution of sulfuric acid (H_2SO_4) is labeled with specific gravity 1.84 and assay (percent purity) 97%. These numbers indicate that 1 ml of this solution weighs 1.84 g and that 97% of the solution is pure H_2SO_4. To calculate the number of grams of pure H_2SO_4 that would be in 1 ml of solution, find the product of the specific gravity (1.84) and the assay (97%).

$$1.84 \text{ g/ml} \times .97 = 1.7848 \text{ g/ml pure } H_2SO_4$$

If the number of grams of pure solute needed for the preparation of a specific solution has been calculated, that number can be divided by the product of the specific gravity and the assay to determine how many ml of the solution on hand will be needed to prepare the desired solution.

$$\frac{\text{Grams of Solute Needed}}{(\text{Specific Gravity})(\text{Assay})} = \text{ml of Concentrated Solution Needed}$$

MW HCl = 36.5

Example 3.11: To make 500 ml of a 1 N HCl solution, 18.25 g of pure HCl is needed. A solution of HCl on the shelf is labeled specific gravity 1.19 and assay 38%. How many milliliter of the stock solution will be needed to prepare the desired solution.

$$\frac{\text{grams of solute needed}}{(\text{specific gravity})(\text{assay})} = \text{ml of concentrated solution}$$

$$\frac{18.25 \text{ g}}{(1.19 \text{ g/ml})(.38)} = x$$

$$40.36 \text{ ml} = x$$

Therefore, 40.36 ml of the stock HCl solution diluted up to 500 ml will produce the desired 1 N HCl solution.

In the preparation of solutions that are corrosive such as acids or bases, it is usually impractical as well as hazardous to measure the amount of solute needed using mass. Preparing solutions using a volume of concentrate diluted up to a total volume is a much easier laboratory procedure. Stock solutions of concentrated acids or bases have labels that give the specific gravity and assay for the concentrate. These concentrates are used to make weaker acid or base solutions. The number of ml of concentrate needed to prepare a solution of a specified concentration can be calculated as illustrated in the following example.

Example 3.12: How many milliliters of a stock HCl solution labeled specific gravity 1.19 and assay 38% will be needed to prepare 2 L of a 1.5 N HCl solution.

1. Calculate the number of grams of pure HCl needed for 2 L of a 1.5 N solution set.

Formula: Equivalent × N × Volume in = grams needed
  Weight   Liters   for solution

$$\frac{36.5 \text{ g}}{\text{eq}} \times 1.5 \frac{\text{eq}}{\text{L}} \times 2 \text{ L} = x$$

109.5 g of pure HCL needed = x

NOTES

36.5/1 = 36.5 eq wt

$\frac{36.5 g}{eq}$ × 1N × .5L =

18.25 g w

500 ml =

1N soln.

---

2. Calculate the g/ml of pure HCl in the stock solution.

   (specific gravity)(assay) = (1.19)(.38) = 0.4522 g HCl/ml

3. Calculate the number of milliliters of stock solution needed to give the desired number of grams of pure solute.

$$\frac{\text{grams of solute needed}}{\text{(specific gravity)(assay)}} = \frac{109.5 \text{ g}}{0.4522 \text{ g/ml}} = 242.15 \text{ ml of concentrated solution}$$

   Therefore, 242.15 ml of the stock solution diluted up to 2 liters will produce a 1.5 N HCl solution.

Practice Problem Set 3.6:

1. How much pure nitric acid (HNO_3) is in 50 ml of concentrated acid if the label specifies a specific gravity of 1.42 and an assay 70% ?

2. What volume of concentrated HCl is required to prepare 1.5 L of a 2 M solution? (specific gravity = 1.19, assay = 38%)

3. Find the specific gravity of a solution if 4.5 ml weighs 6.8 g.

4. What is the molarity and normality of concentrated H_3PO_4 with specific gravity 1.06 and assay 100%?

5. A commercial solution of nitric acid (HNO_3) has density of 1.39 and is 71% pure. What is the molarity of this acid?

6. Make 500 ml of 0.5 N H_3PO_4 (specific gravity 1.16, assay 40%).

7. A small volume, 50 ml, of a solution weighs 275 g. What is the specific gravity of this solution.

8. How many ml of a HCl solution (specific gravity 1.19, 37% assay) would be needed to prepare 2 L of 0.5 N solution?

9. A urine specimen (45 ml) weighs 55.8 g. What is the specific gravity of the urine?

10. Explain in your own words what it means if a solution has a specific gravity of 1.65. What information does the assay give concerning the solution?

NOTES

$H_3PO_4 = 98g\ MW$

$98/3 = 32.7\ eq\ wt$

$32.7 \times .5N \times .5 =$

$\dfrac{8.2g}{(1.16)(.40)} = 17.6\ mL$

NOTES

3.7 PREPARATION OF SOLUTIONS FROM STOCK SOLUTIONS

Many times a new solution is made by adding more solvent to an existing stock solution. These stock solutions may be kept on hand in a laboratory for the preparation of similar solutions having weaker concentrations. This preparation of a weaker solution from a stronger one is nothing more than a dilution of the original solution. The relationship between these two solutions can be expressed using the following formula:

$$V_1 \times C_1 = V_2 \times C_2$$

The volume of the first solution (V_1) times the concentration of the first solution (C_1) equals the volume of the second solution (V_2) times the concentration of the second solution (C_2).

The preparation of a solution in this manner involves the use of a small amount of highly concentrated solution to which more solvent (or diluent) is added. This produces a greater volume of solution and a reduced concentration of the solute. Although the amount of solute has remained constant, the **relative** amounts of the solute and solvent have changed producing the change in concentration. Be sure that all volume and concentration units are the same when using this formula.

Example 3.13: You have 25 ml of a 9% saline solution. How much 5% solution can be produced using 25 ml of the 9%?

Solution #1 = solution on hand = 25 ml of 9%

Solution #2 = new solution being made = x ml of 5%

Solution On Hand = Solution Needed

$$V_1 \times C_1 = V_2 \times C_2$$

$$(25 \text{ ml})(9\%) = (x \text{ ml})(5\%)$$

$$\frac{(25 \text{ ml})(9\%)}{5\%} = x \text{ ml}$$

$$45 \text{ ml} = x$$

Therefore, 25 ml of 9% saline will produce 45 ml of a new solution whose concentration is 5%. (This will be done by adding 20 ml of water to the 25 ml of 9% thereby increasing the volume and decreasing the concentration.)

Example 3.14: How much of a 25 M stock solution would be needed to produce 500 ml of a 10 M solution.

Solution #1 = solution on hand = x ml of 25 M stock solution

Solution #2 = new solution being made = 500 ml of 10 M

Solution On Hand = Solution Needed

$$V_1 \times C_1 = V_2 \times C_2$$

$$(x \text{ ml})(25 \text{ M}) = (500 \text{ ml})(10 \text{ M})$$

$$x \text{ ml} = \frac{(500 \text{ ml})(10 \text{ M})}{25 \text{ M}}$$

$$x = 200 \text{ ml}$$

Therefore, 200 ml of the 25 M stock solution will be needed to produce 500 ml of a 10 M solution.

or

200 ml of 25 M stock solution ⇧ 500 ml ⇨ 500 ml of a 10 M solution

NOTES

NOTES

Since the previous procedures involve the dilution of existing solutions to produce new solutions, it is not possible to begin with a weak solution and make a stronger solution. However, mathematically, an answer can be calculated using the above formula. This answer, on the other hand, is meaningless if you understand the procedure you are following to change the concentrations. The answer will ask you to dilute up to a lesser volume than you have to start with - an impossibility!

Example 3.15: How much 7.5 N solution can be made with 150 ml of 5 N solution?

Solution #1 = solution on hand = 150 ml of 5 N

Solution #2 = new solution being made = x ml of 7.5 N

Solution On Hand   =   Solution Needed

$$V_1 \times C_1 \ = \ V_2 \times C_2$$

$$(150 \text{ ml})(5 \text{ N}) \ = \ (x \text{ ml}) (7.5 \text{ N})$$

$$\frac{(150 \text{ ml}) (5 \cancel{N})}{7.5 \cancel{N}} \ = \ x \text{ ml}$$

$$100 \text{ ml} \ = \ x$$

The formula has produced a numerical answer which asks you to take 150 ml of 5 N and dilute up to 100 ml. This is not possible since you cannot dilute up to a lesser volume.

The $V_1 \times C_1 = V_2 \times C_2$ formula can also be applied to acid and base solutions which neutralize each other. In order for a base to neutralize an acid (or vice versa), the product of the volume and concentration of the base must equal the product of the volume and concentration of the acid. Be sure that the concentration units are given in normality, however, because of the chemical reaction that occurs in neutralization. Equal amounts of a 1 M acid solution and 1 M base will not always neutralize each other because of the combinations of hydrogen and hydroxyl ions that occur. A 1 M solution of an acid with a valence of +2 such as H_2SO_4 will not neutralize an equal amount of a 1 M NaOH solution. The conversion to normality using equivalent weight takes into account the chemical combinations needed for neutralization to occur. Conversion of molarity to normality will be discussed in Section 3.8.

Example 3.16: How much 2 N sulfuric acid is needed to neutralize 180 ml of a 2.5 N sodium hydroxide base?

Since both concentration units are expressed in normality, the $V_1 \times C_1$ formula can be used.

$$
\begin{array}{cc}
V_1 \times C_1 & = \quad V_2 \times C_2 \\
\text{acid} & \text{base}
\end{array}
$$

$$(x \text{ ml}) (2 \text{ N}) = (180 \text{ ml}) (2.5 \text{ N})$$

$$x = \frac{(180 \text{ ml})(2.5 \text{ N})}{2 \text{ N}}$$

$$x = 225 \text{ ml}$$

Therefore, 225 ml of a 2 N sulfuric acid solution will neutralize 180 ml of a 2.5 N sodium hydroxide base.

MIXING SEVERAL SOLUTIONS

When two or more solutions are mixed together, a new solution having a new volume and concentration is produced. Using the $V_1 \times C_1 = V_2 \times C_2$ procedure, we can express the results of this mixture of solutions using the following formula:

$$(V_1 \times C_1) + (V_2 \times C_2) + (V_3 \times C_3) + ... = V_F \times C_F$$

NOTES

NOTES

The unknown V_F is the final volume of the mixture and is the sum of the volumes of the individual solutions that are being combined. Remember that all solutions in the problem must use the same volume units and concentration units.

Example 3.17: What will be the concentration of a solution that is made by mixing 50 ml of a 11 M solution and 25 ml of a 5 M solution?

V_F = total volume of new solution = 50 ml + 25 ml = 75 ml

$$(V_1 \times C_1) + (V_2 \times C_2) = V_F \times C_F$$

$$(50 \text{ ml})(11 \text{ M}) + (25 \text{ ml})(5 \text{ M}) = (75 \text{ ml})(x)$$

$$550 + 125 = 75x$$

$$675 = 75x$$

$$9 = x$$

Therefore, a mixture of 50 ml of the 11 M and 25 ml of the 5 M has produced 75 ml of a solution whose concentration is 9 M.

Example 3.18: How much 9% HCl must be mixed with 4% HCl to produce 50 ml of 6% solution?

$$V_F = V_1 + V_2 = 50 \text{ ml}$$

Since we do not know either of the individual volumes,

$$\text{let } V_1 = x \text{ ml}$$

$$\text{Then, } x + V_2 = 50 \text{ ml}$$

$$\text{and } V_2 = (50 - x) \text{ ml}$$

$$(V_1 \times C_1) + (V_2 \times C_2) = V_F \times C_F$$

$$(x \text{ ml})(9\%) + (50 - x)\text{ml}(4\%) = (50 \text{ ml})(6\%)$$

$$9x + 200 - 4x = 300$$

$$5x = 100$$

$$x = 20 \text{ ml}$$

$$V_1 = x = 20 \text{ ml}$$

$$V_2 = 50 - x = 50 - 20 = 30 \text{ ml}$$

Therefore, 20 ml of 9% HCl + 30 ml of 4% HCl will produce 50 ml of a 6% HCl solution.

NOTES

NOTES

Practice Problem Set 3.7:

1. How much 25% alcohol is needed to make 500 ml of 15% alcohol?

2. How much 0.4 M solution can be made from 50 ml of 1.5 M solution?

3. How much water would be needed to make 50 ml of 10% from 25%?

4. You could make 75 ml of 20% from 25 ml of what %?

5. How much 20% solution is required to make 200 ml of 3% solution?

6. You have a stock solution of 2.5 N H_2SO_4 and need to make 200 ml of a 2 N solution. How much water would be required?

7. How much 9% solution is needed to make 50 ml of 10.5% solution?

8. You could make 150 ml of 0.2% from 5 ml of what percent?

9. You mix 25 ml of 6 N and 75 ml of 4 N NaOH in a flask. What is the concentration of the final solution?

10. You have a 20% saline solution on hand. You need to make 100 ml of a 4% solution. How will you prepare this solution?

11. Twenty milliliters of 6 N HCl is mixed with 80 milliliters of another HCl solution. The resulting mixture has a concentration 3 N. What is the concentration of the second solution that was used for the mixture?

12. Using 3 ml of a concentrated solution, you produce 90 ml of a solution having a concentration 0.5%. What was the concentration of the original solution?

13. How much water should be added to 10 ml of a 6.5 N acid solution to produce a 4 N solution?

14. How much 15% HCl must be mixed with 7% HCl to produce 60 ml of 9% HCl?

15. Explain the procedure for preparing 500 ml of a 1.5 M solution using a concentrated solution that is 12 M.

16. How much of a 2 N NaOH solution will be required to neutralize 50 ml of a 2.5 N H_2SO_4 solution?

17. It requires 50 ml of a 2 N HCl solution to neutralize 20 ml of a NaOH solution. What is the concentration of the base?

18. In a titration procedure 25 ml of 1.2 N solution was required to titrate 10 ml of an unknown solution. What is the normality of the unknown solution?

19. You are given 1.5 L of approximately 0.6 N HCl. For the procedure you are going to do, the acid must be exactly 0.6 N, so 30 ml of the solution is removed and titrated. It is determined to be 0.65 N. How much water should be added to the remaining HCl to make exactly 0.6 N?

NOTES

3.8 CONVERSIONS FROM ONE EXPRESSION OF CONCENTRATION TO ANOTHER

In a laboratory procedure, a problem may occur if the procedure you are required to do calls for a solution with a specific concentration unit and the materials you have on hand have concentration expressed using different units. For example, a procedure may call for 0.5 M NaOH and you have on hand 10% NaOH. In order to complete the procedure, a conversion of concentration units will be necessary. The following formulas should help in converting one type of concentration unit to another.

$$\% \leftrightarrow \text{N, M}$$

In converting from % to normality or molarity, the definitions of these concentrations must be considered. Percent is defined to be grams per 100 ml while molarity and normality are based on grams per liter (1000 ml). Only $\%^{w/v}$ can be converted to molarity or normality since these concentrations are by definition weight per unit volume measurements.

The conversion formulas are derived as follows:

$$M = \frac{g/L}{\text{molecular weight}} \qquad N = \frac{g/L}{\text{equivalent weight}}$$

$$M = \frac{g/100\,ml \times 10}{\text{molecular weight}} \qquad N = \frac{g/100\,ml \times 10}{\text{equivalent weight}}$$

$$M = \frac{\% \times 10}{\text{molecular weight}} \qquad N = \frac{\% \times 10}{\text{equivalent weight}}$$

In the numerator of each fraction, the number of grams of solute that would be in a liter of solution is calculated from the % concentration and then divided by the molecular or equivalent weight depending upon the desired concentration unit.

Example 3.19: Convert 10% NaCl to molarity.

molecular weight of NaCl = 58.5 g

$$M = \frac{\% \times 10}{\text{molecular weight}}$$

$$M = \frac{10 \times 10}{58.5}$$

$$M = 1.71$$

Therefore, 10% NaCl = 1.71 M NaCl

Example 3.20: Convert 2.5 N H_2SO_4 to %.

molecular weight of H_2SO_4 = 98 g

equivalent weight of H_2SO_4 = 49 g

$$N = \frac{\% \times 10}{\text{equivalent weight}}$$

$$2.5 = \frac{\% \times 10}{49}$$

$$(2.5)\,(49) = \% \times 10$$

$$122.5 = \% \times 10$$

$$\frac{122.5}{10} = \%$$

$$12.25 = \%$$

Therefore, 2.5 N H_2SO_4 = 12.25% H_2SO_4

NOTES

NOTES

M ↔ N

Molarity and normality are very similar concentration units differing only in the weights used (molecular weight vs equivalent weight). The equivalent weight is calculated by dividing the molecular weight by the positive valence of the compound being considered. Therefore, we can derive the conversion formulas as follows:

Since

$$\text{molecular weight} \times M = g/L$$
$$\text{and}$$
$$\text{equivalent weight} \times N = g/L$$

Then

$$\text{molecular weight} \times M = \text{equivalent weight} \times N$$

$$\text{molecular weight} \times M = \frac{\text{molecular weight}}{\text{positive valence}} \times N$$

$$\frac{(\text{positive valence}) \,(\cancel{\text{molecular weight}}) \,(M)}{\cancel{\text{molecular weight}}} = N$$

$$\textbf{(positive valence) (M)} = \textbf{N}$$

Solving this equation for molarity results in the formula:

$$\textbf{M} = \frac{\textbf{N}}{\text{positive valence}}$$

Example 3.21: Convert 2.5 M H_3PO_4 to normality.

$$N = \text{positive valence} \times M$$

$$N = 3 \times 2.5$$

$$N = 7.5$$

Therefore, 2.5 M H_3PO_4 = 7.5 N H_3PO_4.

---

mg/dl ↔ mEq/L

Another type of conversion that may be necessary is a conversion of milligrams per deciliter to milliequivalents per liter or vice versa. This conversion, like the conversion involving percents, involves a change in volume units as well as the inclusion of the equivalent weight of the compound. The conversion formula can be derived as follows. Recall that:

$$\text{mEq/L} = \frac{\text{mg/L}}{\text{equivalent weight}}$$

Since mg/dl = mg/100 ml, the number of mg/L can be found by multiplying mg/100 ml × 10. Therefore,

$$\text{mEq/L} = \frac{\text{mg/100 ml} \times 10}{\text{equivalent weight}}$$

$$\textbf{mEq/L} = \frac{\textbf{mg/dl} \times \textbf{10}}{\textbf{equivalent weight}}$$

Example 3.22: Convert 350 mg/dl NaCl to mEq/L.

$$\text{mEq/L} = \frac{\text{mg/dl} \times 10}{\text{equivalent weight}}$$

$$\text{mEq/L} = \frac{350 \times 10}{58.5}$$

$$\text{mEq/L} = \frac{3500}{58.5}$$

$$\text{mEq/L} = 59.83$$

Therefore, 350 mg/dl NaCl = 59.83 mEg/L NaCl

NOTES

Example 3.23: Express 125 mEq/L NaOH as mg/dl NaOH.

$$\text{mEq/L} \;=\; \frac{\text{mg/dl} \times 10}{\text{equivalent weight}}$$

$$125 \;=\; \frac{\text{mg/dl} \times 10}{40}$$

$$125 \times 40 \;=\; \text{mg/dl} \times 10$$

$$5000 \;=\; \text{mg/dl} \times 10$$

$$500 \;=\; \text{mg/dl}$$

Therefore,

$$125 \text{ mEq/L NaOH} \;=\; 500 \text{ mg/dl NaOH}.$$

---

mg/dl ↔ mmol/L

The trend in clinical laboratories is to report all quantitative units in SI (Système International d'Unités) units for uniformity. Since the mole is one of the basic units in the SI system, concentrations given in mg/dl may need to be converted to mmol/L. The formula for this conversion is much like the preceding one but is based on the molecular weight of the compound involved.

$$\text{mmol/L} \;=\; \frac{\text{mg/100 ml} \times 10}{\text{molecular weight}}$$

$$\textbf{mmol/L} \;=\; \frac{\textbf{mg/dl} \times \textbf{10}}{\textbf{molecular weight}}$$

Example 3.24: Convert 368 mg/dl sodium to mmol/L.

molecular weight of sodium = 23 g

$$\text{mmol/L} = \frac{\text{mg/dl} \times 10}{\text{molecular weight}}$$

$$\text{mmol/L} = \frac{368 \times 10}{23}$$

$$\text{mmol/L} = \frac{3680}{23}$$

$$\text{mmol/L} = 160$$

Therefore,

$$368 \text{ mg/dl sodium} = 160 \text{ mmol/L}.$$

The preceding conversion formulas can be used for most conversions that would be needed in a lab. Remember that if you are using the $V_1 \times C_1 = V_2 \times C_2$ equation in working with solutions, the concentration units must be alike. Depending on the concentration units given in the problem, a conversion may be necessary before you can use the formula.

Example 3.25: Make 350 ml of 6 N NaOH from 25%$^{w/v}$.

This problem calls for the use of the $V_1 \times C_1 = V_2 \times C_2$ formula but the concentrations given are in different units. A conversion of N to % or % to N must be done. Mathematically, it does not matter which unit of concentration (N or %) is calculated as long as the same units are used in the $V_1 \times C_1$ formula.

$$N = \frac{\% \times 10}{\text{equivalent weight}}$$

$$N = \frac{25 \times 10}{40}$$

$$N = \frac{250}{40}$$

$$N = 6.25$$

NOTES

Now using the $V_1 \times C_1$ formula, we can calculate the amount of 6.25 N NaOH (25%$^{w/v}$) needed to make 350 ml of a 6 N NaOH solution.

$$V_1 \times C_1 = V_2 \times C_2$$

$$(x\ ml)\ (6.25\ N) = (350\ ml)\ (6\ N)$$

$$6.25x = 2100$$

$$x = \frac{2100}{6.25}$$

$$x = 336\ ml$$

Therefore, 336 ml of 25%$^{w/v}$ NaOH ⇧ 350 ml ⇨ 350 ml of 6 N NaOH.

Practice Problem Set 3.8:

1. What is the normality of a 1.5% saline solution?

2. You have a 70%$^{w/v}$ HNO_3 solution. Express its concentration as molarity and as normality.

3. Convert 6 M NaOH to percent.

4. A sodium concentration reported is 325 mg/dl. What is the concentration in milliequivalents per liter?

5. Express 80 mEq/L NaCl as milligrams NaCl per deciliter.

6. What molarity is equal to 6 N H_2SO_4?

7. Express as mmol/L:

   a. 25 mg/dl of calcium
   b. 75 mg/dl of glucose (mol.wt. = 180)

8. How much 6 N HCl could be made from 20 ml of 12 M HCl?

9. How much 20%$^{w/v}$ H_2SO_4 can be made with 50 ml of 6.2 N H_2SO_4?

10. Give the concentration of a 2% $CaCl_2$ solution in normality and molarity.

11. How much of a 2 M NaOH solution will be required to neutralize 50 ml of a 2.5 M H_2SO_4 solution? (Remember that concentrations must be expressed in normality when considering acid-base neutralization.)

NOTES

CHAPTER SUMMARY

KEY TERMS TO REMEMBER

solute   solvent
molarity   normality
mole   equivalent
millimole   milliequivalent
gram molecular weight   equivalent weight
specific gravity   density

FORMULAS

Molarity (M) = $\dfrac{\text{moles}}{\text{liter}}$ = $\dfrac{\text{millimoles}}{\text{milliliter}}$ = $\dfrac{\text{g/L}}{\text{molecular weight}}$

(molecular weight)(M)(volume in L) = grams solute needed for solution

Normality (N) = $\dfrac{\text{equivalents}}{\text{liter}}$ = $\dfrac{\text{milliequivalent}}{\text{milliliter}}$ = $\dfrac{\text{g/L}}{\text{equivalent weight}}$

Equivalent Weight = $\dfrac{\text{molecular weight}}{\text{positive valence}}$

(equivalent weight)(N)(volume in L) = grams solute needed for solution

Using Specific Gravity

$\dfrac{\text{grams of solute needed}}{\text{(specific gravity)(assay)}}$ = ml of concentrate needed

$V_1 \times C_1 = V_2 \times C_2$ - for making a new solution from one with a given concentration

$V_1 C_1 + V_2 C_2 + \ldots = V_F C_F$ - for mixing several solutions of varying concentrations

Conversions -

$M = \dfrac{\% \times 10}{\text{molecular weight}}$ $N = \dfrac{\% \times 10}{\text{equivalent weight}}$

$M = \dfrac{N}{\text{positive valence}}$ $N = (\text{positive valence})(M)$

$\text{mmol/L} = \dfrac{\text{mg/dl} \times 10}{\text{molecular weight}}$

$\text{mEq/L} = \dfrac{\text{mg/dl} \times 10}{\text{equivalent weight}}$

CHAPTER REVIEW PROBLEMS

1. How much 15% solution can be made from 42 g of NaCl?

2. a. How many grams of NaCl will be needed to make 250 ml of a 15%$^{w/v}$ saline solution?

    b. How would you make 500 g of a 10%$^{w/w}$ NaCl aqueous solution?

3. Convert 500 mg NaCl/200 ml to the following concentration units:
    a. %   b. M   c. N

4. How many grams of NaOH are in 1.5 L of a 12% solution?

5. Five ml of HCl will make 75 ml of a solution having what percent concentration?

6. How would you make 200 ml of a 4% solution of alcohol by using a stock solution that is 50% alcohol?

7. How much water should be added to make 30 ml of a 1.5 N HCl from a 1 N HCl standard?

8. You have on hand 2500 ml of an H_2SO_4 stock solution of unknown concentration. You discover that 25 ml of this acid solution will be neutralized by 20 ml of a 5 N NaOH solution. How much water will need to be added to the remainder of the H_2SO_4 solution in order to make it 1.5 N?

9. In a titration procedure, 20 ml of 1.2 N solution was required to titrate 4 ml of an unknown solution. What is the normality of the unknown solution?

10. You have on hand a 12% saline solution and a 20% saline solution. You are told to make 500 ml of a 15% saline. How much of each solution will you need to use to make this 15% saline solution?

NOTES

11. How much 6 N HCL must be mixed with 4 N HCL to produce 100 ml of 4.6 N HCL solution?

12. a. By definition, a 2.5 M solution contains _____.
    In 1 liter of a 2.5 M H_3PO_4 solution, there are _____g of H_3PO_4.

    b. A 0.25 N solution contains _____ milliequivalents per liter and _____ milliequivalents per milliliter.

13. There are 200 g of NaOH per 350 ml of solution. What is the molarity?

14. What weight of NaOH is required to prepare 3000 ml of a 0.7 M solution?

15. What is the molarity of a solution of Na_2SO_4 in which 284 g of this salt are placed in 500.0 ml of water?

16. How many nanograms of H_3PO_4 would 40 ml of a 1×10^{-6} N solution contain?

17. There are 150 mEq NaOH/500 ml in a solution. What is the normality of the solution?

18. a. A solution of 250 ml of 2.5 N $CaCl_2$ solution contains how many milliequivalents?

    b. What is the weight of the $CaCL_2$ in this solution?

19. Outline the steps you would take in preparing 500 ml of a 1.5 N HCl solution.

20. If 25 g of Na_2CO_3 are diluted to 1250 ml, what is the concentration in terms of:

    a. molarity

    b. normality

    c. %$^{w/v}$

21. You have 50 ml of H_2SO_4 (specific gravity 1.84, assay 95.5%) diluted up to 250 ml. Give the following:

    a. %$^{v/v}$ c. molarity

    b. %$^{w/v}$ d. normality

22. How would you make 1 L of 6 M nitric acid (HNO_3)? (specific gravity 1.42, assay 73%)

23. a. What molarity equals 15%$^{w/v}$ NaCl?

    b. What %$^{w/v}$ is equal to 11 N NaOH?

24. Convert 25 mg/dl NaCl to:

    a. mEq/L

    b. mmol/L

25. How much 6 N H_3PO_4 can be made from 20 ml of 3 M H_3PO_4?

26. The results of a test for potassium in a urine specimen were 725 mEq K/L. Express these units as:

    a. mg/dl   b. mmol/L   c. normality

NOTES

SUGGESTED LABORATORY EXERCISES

LABORATORY EXERCISE 1: MIXING SOLUTIONS

This is a simple laboratory exercise designed to have students make two solutions having the same concentration but different volumes. The purpose is to demonstrate that concentration is a <u>relative</u> measurement and not dependent on the volume prepared.

Equipment and Chemicals Needed:
➢ Granulated sugar (sucrose, $C_{12}H_{22}O_{11}$), pure water, scales that measure in grams, 2 graduated cylinders.

Procedure:
1. Calculate the number of grams of sucrose needed to make 50 ml of a 25%$^{w/v}$ sucrose solution.

2. Measure the calculated amount of sugar using the scales and place in one graduated cylinder.

3. Add water to the sucrose diluting up to a total volume of 50 ml. Mix well.

4. In the second graduated cylinder, prepare 100 ml of a 25%$^{w/v}$ sucrose solution using the same steps you have just followed.

5. Take a drop from the first tube (50 ml) and taste it (it's just sugar water!). Then sample a drop from the second mixture (100 ml). (Be sure they have been thoroughly mixed.) Do the two solutions taste equally sweet? Though not a precise measuring instrument, your tongue should tell you that the concentrations of the two solutions are the same even though the volumes of the two are different. The ratios of sucrose. and water in the two solutions are the same resulting in like concentrations.

LABORATORY EXERCISE 2: SPECIFIC GRAVITY

NOTES

This laboratory exercise can be done as a follow-up to Laboratory Exercise 1 or as a separate activity. A solution is prepared and its mass obtained. A comparison is then made of the actual mass and the theoretical mass indicated by the specific gravity.

Equipment and Chemicals Needed:
➤ Granulated sugar (sucrose, $C_{12}H_{22}O_{11}$), pure water, graduated cylinder, scales that measure in grams.

Procedure:
1. Prepare 100 ml of a sucrose solution having a concentration of $25\%^{w/v}$.

2. Calculate the weight of 100 ml of a $25\%^{w/v}$ sucrose solution using its specific gravity 1.1036.[*]

3. Now obtain the mass in grams of the solution you have prepared. Be sure to discount the weight of the container.

4. Is the actual mass the same as the calculated mass? Is it close? If the actual mass is not exactly the same, why do you think it is different?

5. Repeat the exercise with different concentrations or solutes.

   a. $50\%^{w/v}$ sucrose solution   specific gravity = 1.2296

   b. $20\%^{w/v}$ salt (NaCl) solution   specific gravity = 1.1978

[*] Note: Specific gravity values for various common standard solutions can be obtained from any one of several handbooks of chemistry or physics.

NOTES

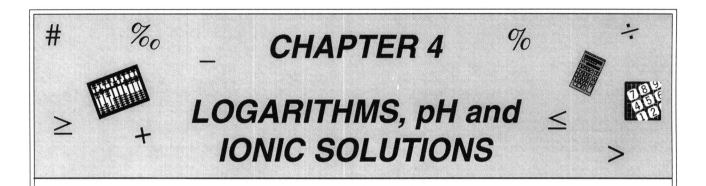

In This Chapter:

In this chapter the student will learn about logarithms, how to manipulate common logarithmic equation forms, solve basic equations involving logarithms and how logarithms are used in the laboratory as related to applications involving pH measurements. The proper use of a scientific calculator to calculate logarithmic values will also be included. It is assumed that the student has already had at least one basic chemistry course, so common chemistry terms and symbology will not be explained.

NOTES

4.1 INTRODUCTION - LOGARITHMS

A **logarithm** is not a number in the usual sense. As you will learn in section 4.2, it is really an **exponent**. In working with equations or formulas that use logarithms, certain standard abbreviations are used. The word *logarithm* and the phrase *logarithm of* are both abbreviated **log** or **ln**. These two abbreviations have different meanings that will be discussed in this chapter.

Logarithms are used frequently in laboratory work. The pH, pOH and pK scales, plotting of standard curves, radioactive decay rates and half-life calculations for radioactive tracers and elements, and population growth rates are all examples of areas where logarithms are used. To be a competent laboratory technician, you will need to be familiar with logarithms and their applications in the laboratory environment. In this chapter you will learn the basic manipulations and procedures that are necessary for dealing with logarithms.

As a student, you may think that logarithms are some new, diabolical form of mathematics designed to confuse and confound laboratory technicians. Logarithms themselves are nothing new. A mathematician named John Napier is credited for their invention. He first described them in his book, *A Description of the Wonderful Law of Logarithms*, published in 1614.

In solving problems and doing basic calculations in this chapter, it is assumed that you will have access to a scientific calculator that has logarithm function keys. To be sure that your calculator can be used, look for keys that are labeled **log** and **ln**. These two keys are side by side on most calculators, regardless of the brand. If your calculator has such keys, then you are ready to do all of the problems and applications in this chapter.

Tables of logarithms are available and may be used. However, they are cumbersome for day to day use in a laboratory setting. Instructions for using your calculator to perform necessary calculations will be included in this chapter.

4.2 LOGARITHIC EQUATION FORMS

Equations that involve the use of logarithms and exponents may be written in two different forms. These forms are **exponential form** and **logarithmic form**. In this section you will learn how to write equations in both of these forms. You will find that, with a little practice, manipulating these two equation forms is easy to do.

EXPONENTIAL FORM
$$b^x = y$$

An equation written in **exponential form** has a base number with an exponent (sometimes called a power) that is a variable. As shown above, 'b' is the **base**. This base number has an **exponent** denoted by 'x.' Using the letter 'x' indicates that the exponent (or power) is a **variable**. This equation says that if you raise 'b' to the 'xth' power, then the result will be equal to the number 'y'.

You may already be familiar with equations in which numbers have exponents. For example, in a basic algebra class you may have solved equations like $x^2 = 9$. Solving this type of equation is fairly simple. The question posed by this equation is, "What number squared (that is, multiplied by itself) equals 9?" With a little thought it can be seen that $x = 3$. In this type of equation, the variable (x) is raised to a constant number (2) power.

However, in the exponential form of a logarithmic equation, the **exponent is a variable**. The fact that the variable (unknown number) is in the exponent makes the equation difficult to solve.

Suppose we had an equation like $2^x = 4$. This exponential equation asks "What exponent (or power) must x be so that 2 multiplied times itself x times will equal 4?" Of course it is probably obvious that $x = 2$ ($2^2 = 2 \times 2 = 4$). But, what if we had to solve an equation like $2^x = 5$? The value of x here must be larger than 2, since $2^2 = 4$, and smaller than 3, since $2^3 = 8$. The exponent must have a decimal number value. Before you can solve this type of equation, you must also understand the logarithmic form of these equations.

LOGARITHMIC FORM
$$\log_b y = x$$

This equation is the same as $b^x = y$, but it has been rewritten in **logarithmic form**. The base number from the exponential form is now the base number of the logarithm. The logarithm of the number 'y' is equal to the exponent, 'x', of the original exponential equation. If you read this equation it says, "the logarithm, base number b, of y is equal to x." Whenever you find the value of a logarithm you have answered the question, *"What exponent (or power) must be placed on the base number 'b' so that when multiplied out the result will equal the number 'y'?"*

CHANGING FORMS

Before moving too deeply into the uses of logarithms, you must first learn a few basic techniques for handling logarithms. One of these is switching from exponential form to logarithmic form, and vice versa. What follows are some examples of equations written in both forms. Notice that in each case, the log equals the exponent used in the equivalent exponential form, and the base number of the log is the base number from the exponential form.

EXPONENTIAL FORM	LOGARITHMIC FORM
$2^3 = 8$	$\log_2 8 = 3$
$10^2 = 100$	$\log_{10} 100 = 2$
$9^{1/2} = 3$	$\log_9 3 = \frac{1}{2}$
$4^{-1} = 0.25$	$\log_4 0.25 = -1$
$5^x = 0.2$	$\log_5 0.2 = x$

Example 4.1: Rewrite $5^2 = 25$ in logarithmic form.

STEP A: Note that the base number is 5. This will be the base of the log (logarithm).

STEP B: Note that the exponent on that base is 2. In logarithmic form, the log will equal 2.

STEP C: Write the equation: $\log_5 25 = 2$.

If you read this equation it says, "the log, base 5, of 25 is 2."
You could also say that the exponent that must be placed on a
base of 5 so that it will multiply out to be 25 is 2.

NOTES

NOTES

Practice Problem Set 4.2:

A: Rewrite each of the following in the equivalent logarithmic form.

1. $10^x = 75$
2. $5^2 = x$
3. $e^x = 42.4$
4. $x^5 = 500$
5. $10^3 = x$

6. $e^{1/2} = x$
7. $x^a = B$
8. $169^{1/2} = x$
9. $10^{-4} = x$
10. $e^x = 2/3$

11. $3^2 = 9$
12. $(-3)^3 = -27$
13. $10^3 = 1000$
14. $e^0 = 1$
15. $(1/2)^3 = 1/8$

B: Rewrite each of the following in the equivalent exponential form.

1. $\log_5 25 = x$
2. $\log_{10} x = 2$
3. $\log_{-3}(-8) = x$
4. $\log_x 3.65 = 4$
5. $\log_x A = C$

6. $\log_{1/2} x = 20$
7. $\log_e 40 = x$
8. $\log_e x = 2.49$
9. $\log_{10} 2 = x$
10. $\log_2 x = 9$

11. $\log_{10} 100 = 2$
12. $\log_e 2.71828 = 1$
13. $\log_5 125 = 3$
14. $\log_2 32 = 5$
15. $\log_{400} 20 = 1/2$

4.3 COMMON LOGARITHMS

It is true that logarithms can have any base number. However, for all uses in the chemistry lab, only two bases need to be considered. These two base numbers are 10 and 2.718281828459045... No, that second base number is not a typographical error; it really is a long, messy decimal number. We will discuss these bases and how to use your calculator to do any necessary calculations.

Logs with a base number of 10 are called **common logs**. Since this base is so frequently used, we will abbreviate our logarithmic notation as follows:

$$\log_{10} = \log$$

If no base number is written as a subscript on the 'log,' then the base number is understood to be 10. Thus, 'log 100' is the base 10 log of 100.

Example 4.2: Find the base 10 log of 100; log 100 = __x__ .

> This problem is asking you what exponent must be placed on a base of 10 so that the multiplied answer will equal 100. Let's use a calculator to solve this problem.
>
> **STANDARD CALCULATOR PROCEDURE:**
> First find the key labeled 'log.' On a standard calculator you must first enter the number that you want to find the log for, so enter '100' and press the 'log' key (the sequence is '100 log'). At this point your calculator should display the number 2. Thus, log 100 = 2. If we had rewritten the equation in logarithmic form it would have been $10^x = 100$. Then, the question to be answered is,"10 to what power equals 100?" The answer that your calculator gave you is correct; $10^2 = 100$, so the x = 2.
>
> Therefore, log 100 = 2.

NOTES

DIRECT ENTRY CALCULATOR PROCEDURE:

With a direct entry calculator, first press the 'log' key and then enter '100'. Next you must press the 'enter' key (the sequence is 'log 100 enter'). At this point the calculator should display the number 2. In other words, $10^2 = 100$.

So again, log 100 = 2.

There are many different brand names of calculators available, but they will work using one of the two methods shown above. Find out which one works for your particular calculator and then follow the same procedure each time.

Example 4.3: Find the value of the following: log 300 = x

Enter '300' followed by the 'log' key. You should see 2.477121255, approximately, on your calculator. (Or enter 'log 300 enter' on a direct entry calculator.)

So, log 300 = 2.477121255.

Example 4.4: Find the value of the following: log 10 000 = x

Enter '10 000 log' on your calculator. You should see 4 displayed as the answer. In other words, 10 to what power equals 10 000? $10^4 = 10\ 000$.

So, log 10 000 = 4.

IMPORTANT NOTE: There is a problem that you may encounter with finding the value of logarithms, though this should be in only very rare circumstances in a laboratory situation (usually due to a mistake on your part). The problem is that you cannot find the log of a negative number. If you were asked to find 'log(-100)' you could not because there is no answer to this situation and a calculator will display E indicating that an error has occurred.

Example 4.5: Find, log(-50).

Enter '50' followed by the sign change key '±' and then 'log' (or 'log ± 50 enter' on a direct entry calculator). Instead of giving you a numerical value, your calculator will tell you that an error has been made. You have asked the calculator to do something that it cannot do.

Therefore, log(-50) = undefined.

NOTES

NOTES

Practice Problem Set 4.3:

Find each of the following common logs with your calculator.

1. log 100 =

2. log 1000 =

3. log 25 =

4. log 4.6 =

5. log (-2) =

6. log 0.049 =

7. log 50 000 =

8. log 2.557 =

9. log 1/2 =

10. log 3.45 =

4.4 NATURAL LOGARITHMS

As mentioned in the previous section, there is a second base number that is often used in applications of logarithms. That base is the number 2.718281828459045... Now, that's an awfully long, irrational number. This number was derived from studies of exponential growth and decay of bacteria, radioactive half-lives and similar such natural phenomena. This number is given its own special symbol, *e*. It was given this letter for its symbol to honor a Swiss mathematician named Leonhard Euler (1707-1783). Logs that have the number *e* as their base number are called **natural logarithms**.

$$e = 2.718281828459045...$$

Since this base number is very frequently used in calculations, there is an abbreviation used to stand for base *e* logs.

$$\log_e = \ln$$

If you see 'ln' then the base is understood to be the number represented by *e*. Thus, $\ln 100 = \log_e 100$.

Your calculator will also work problems with natural logs in the same fashion as it does common logs. Find the 'log' key on your calculator and right next to it you will find the 'ln' key.

Example 4.6: Find ln 300.

First enter '300' on your calculator, Next locate and press the 'ln' key (or 'ln 300 enter' on a direct entry calculator). Your calculator should display 5.703782475, approximately.

Therefore, ln 300 = 5.703782475.

NOTES

Practice Problem Set 4.4:

Find each of the following natural logs with your calculator.

1. ln 100 =

2. ln 5 =

3. ln 2.79 =

4. ln (-4.73) =

5. ln e =

6. ln 0 =

7. ln 0.00476 =

8. ln 20 000 =

9. ln 1/4 =

10. ln 1 =

4.5 ANTILOGS

In the previous two sections of this chapter you have been finding the logarithms of numbers. Like most mathematical operations, there is an inverse process. The inverse of finding the log of a number is finding an **antilog**.

Example 4.7: (a) Solve the following: log 100 = x

Enter '100 log' in your calculator and you should see '2' as the answer. Thus, log 100 = 2, so x = 2. As discussed in previous sections, the calculator tells us that 2 is the exponent that must be placed on the base number 10 so that the result of multiplying will equal 100. Or, $10^2 = 100$.

(b) Solve the following: log x = 2.

The question to be answered here is different than in part (a). The base number is 10 and the log equals the exponent that is to be placed on that base. Thus, we have a base of 10 with an exponent of 2, 10^2. To get our calculator to calculate the value of 'x' here, we must do an antilog. On your calculator you must find the 'second function' key (or its equivalent on your calculator). The key may be marked '2nd' or '2^{nd}f'. To find the antilog enter the following sequence, '2 2^{nd}f log ='. The calculator should display '100.'

Another way of indicating that you are to find an antilog is to write 'log^{-1}.' Some brands of calculators will show this on their key pad. Thus there are two ways of indicating that an antilog is to be found:

log x = 2 and log^{-1} 2 = x.

NOTES

Example 4.8: Solve for x:

(a) log x = 0.437

In your calculator enter: 0.437 $2^{nd}f$ log. The result is 2.735268726. Thus,

x = 2.735268726

(b) ln x = 1.34

In your calculator enter: 1.34 $2^{nd}f$ ln. The result is 3.819043505. Thus,

x = 3.819043505

(c) $\ln^{-1} 1.34 = x$

This is exactly the same problem as (b) but it is written in the alternate form. Thus,

x = 3.819043505

Practice Problem Set 4.5:

Find each of the following antilogs with your calculator (i.e., solve for x in each case).

1. $\log x = 4$

2. $\log x = -4$

3. $\ln x = 0.25$

4. $\log x = 2/3$

5. $\ln x = 5.25$

6. $\log x = -0.04$

7. $\log^{-1} 0.535 = x$

8. $\ln^{-1} 2 = x$

9. $\ln x = -0.35$

10. $\log^{-1} 3 = x$

NOTES

4.6 IONIC SOLUTIONS

Logarithms have many applications in a laboratory setting. In this section we will look at some of them. At this point it will be assumed that the student has had a basic course in general chemistry. In that course you should have studied ions and ionic bonds. Ions are attracted to each other in a compound due to their opposite electrical charges. When ionically bonded molecules are dissolved in a solvent, they **dissociate** or **ionize**. This means that the ionic bonds are broken and the solution then contains ions of positive charge and ions of negative charge from the original molecules.

There are three general categories of ionic compounds: **acids, bases and salts**. Acids are compounds that contribute hydrogen ions (H^+), which are free protons, to a solution. Bases are compounds that accept protons from a solution. Salts are compounds that contribute neither free protons nor hydroxyl ions (OH^-) to a solution in which they are dissolved. An acidic solution is one in which there are more H^+ ions than OH^-. A basic (or **alkaline**) solution has more free OH^- ions than it does H^+ ions. If a solution is neutral, then the numbers of H^+ and OH^- ions are equal.

It is important to note that **in all aqueous solutions** (whether they be acid, base or neutral) **the molar concentration of the hydrogen ions multiplied by the molar concentration of the hydroxyl ions will always be equal to 1 X 10^{-14}.** Whenever one wishes to refer to molar concentrations, an abbreviation is used in which brackets are placed around the ion symbol. Thus, $[H^+]$ indicates the molar concentration of hydrogen ions in a solution and $[OH^-]$ the molar concentration of hydroxyl ions. So, the above relationship between the molar masses of the ions can be written as a formula:

$$[H^+] \; X \; [OH^-] = 1 \; X \; 10^{-14}$$

The hydrogen ion concentration depends upon the degree of dissociation (or percent of ionization) that occurs in a given solution. If the percent of ionization is known, as it often is in strongly acidic or basic solutions, then $[H^+]$ can be determined from the normality, N, as follows:

| N X % ionization = [H⁺] | *NOTES* |

Example 4.9: Strong acids will completely dissociate (100% ionization). Thus, the hydrogen ion concentration of a 0.2 N solution of HCl can be easily determined as follows:

N X % ionization = $[H^+]$

$(0.2N)(100\%) = [H^+]$

$(0.2)(1) = [H^+]$

Therefore, $[H^+] = 0.2g\ H^+/L$ in a 0.2 N HCl solution.

Example 4.10: Weak acids will not completely dissociate in solutions. Acetic acid (CH_3COOH) will only slightly dissociate into H^+ ions and CH_3COO^- (acetate) ions. This dissociation may be as little as 1%. Now, calculate the hydrogen ion concentration of a 0.2 N solution of acetic acid.

N X % ionization = $[H^+]$

$(0.2\ N)(1\%) = [H^+]$

$(0.2\ N)(.01) = [H^+]$

Therefore, $[H^+] = 0.002\ g\ H^+/L$ in a 0.2 N acetic acid solution.

NOTES

4.7 pH AND pOH

Using ion concentrations to express the acidity or alkalinity of solutions is often inconvenient. Sorensen developed a scale and created the 'pH' symbology that is now in common use. He called the scale 'pH' since it measures what he called the potential of potency of the hydrogen ions in a solution. The basic definition of pH states that **pH is the logarithm of the reciprocal of [H⁺]**. An alternative way of saying the same thing is **pH is the negative logarithm of [H⁺]**.

The following equations involving both pH and pOH will be very useful:

pH	pOH
pH = log(1/[H⁺])	**pOH = log(1/[OH⁻])**
pH = -log[H⁺]	**pOH = -log[OH⁻]**

The pH scale runs from 0 to 14. Numbers lower than 7 indicate acidic solutions, numbers above 7 indicate alkaline solutions and 7 is neutral. A useful relationship between pH and pOH is:

pH + pOH = 14

Example 4.11: The pH of a certain acid solution is known to be 4.6. What is the pOH of this acid?

$$pH + pOH = 14$$

$$4.6 + pOH = 14$$

$$pOH = 14 - 4.6$$

Therefore, pOH = 9.4

Example 4.12: The hydrogen ion concentration of a certain solution is known to be 1×10^{-3}. What is the pH of this solution?

$$pH = -\log[H^+]$$

$$pH = -[\log (1 \times 10^{-3})]$$

$$pH = -(-3)$$

(Note: in your calculator enter 'log 1 EE 3 +/- =' to get -3)

Therefore, pH = 3

Example 4.13: A solution of 0.3 N acid is known to be 95% ionized. Find each of the following: (a) $[H^+]$, (b) $[OH^-]$, (c) pH and (d) pOH.

(a)   N X % ionization = $[H^+]$
        (0.3 N)(0.95) = $[H^+]$
        $[H^+]$ = 0.285 mol H^+/L (or 2.85×10^{-1} g H^+/L)

(b) $[H^+] \times [OH^-] = 1 \times 10^{-14}$
        $(2.85 \times 10^{-1})([OH^-]) = 1 \times 10^{-14}$
        $[OH^-] = (1 \times 10^{-14})/(2.85 \times 10^{-1})$
        $[OH^-] = 3.51 \times 10^{-14}$ mol OH^-/L

(c) $pH = -\log[H^+]$
        $pH = -\log(2.85 \times 10^{-1})$
        $pH = -(-0.545)$
        $pH = 0.545$

(d)   pH + pOH = 14
        0.545 + pOH = 14
        pOH = 14 - 0.545
        pOH = 13.455

Note: In part (a) of this example, the $[H^+]$ concentration has been expressed as mol/L and then as the same number of grams/L. This is true because 1 mole of hydrogen has a gram molecular weight of 1 gram.

NOTES

NOTES

If an acid or base dissociates completely, (e.g. HCl or NaOH), the preparation of an acid or base solution with a given pH can be done using formulas presented in Chapter 3. The required concentration of the solution is calculated from the pH number designated in the problem.

Example 4.14: Prepare 500 ml of an HCl solution having a pH = 1.5.

HCl is a strong acid that dissociates completely (100%). Therefore, one liter of a 1 M HCl solution contains 1 mole of HCl which is composed of 1 mole of H^+ and 1 mole of Cl^-. Since the molar concentration of H^+ can be derived from the pH number, the molar concentration of the HCL can also be derived from the pH.

Since pH = 1.5, $[HCl] = [H^+] = \log^{-1}(-1.5)$.

$[HCl] = [H^+] = 0.0316$ mol/L

Formula: Mol Weight × M × Volume in L = Grams Needed

36.5 × 0.0316 × 0.500 = grams needed

0.577 = grams needed

Therefore, 0.577g HCl ⇧ 500 ml ⇨ 500 ml of HCl solution (pH = 1.5)

Practice Problem Set 4.7:

Solve each of the following problems.

1. If the pH of a certain solution is 3, then what is the pOH of that solution?

2. What is the pH of a solution with $[OH^-] = 5.2 \times 10^{-7}$?

3. What is the pH of 0.05 M HCl?

4. A certain acid is 1.5 N and is only 20% ionized. Find each of the following:
    (a) $[H^+]$ (b) pH   (c) pOH   (d) $[OH^-]$.

5. To prepare 1500 ml of a solution of NaOH with a pH of 11.5, how many grams of NaOH are needed?

6. In distilled water, the concentration of hydrogen ions is 1×10^{-7}. What is the pH?

7. A certain hair conditioner has a pH of 6. What is the hydrogen ion concentration of the conditioner?

8. Find the pH of milk if $[H^+] = 1.77 \times 10^{-8}$.

9. Find $[H^+]$ if the pH of a glass of wine is 4.75.

10. In a certain solution, $[H^+] = 4.2 \times 10^{-5}$.
    What is (a) its pH and (b) its $[OH^-]$?

NOTES

NOTES

4.8 ACID-BASE RELATIONSHIPS

Acid-base relationships can be rather complicated. The main acid-base relationship in the human body involves the combination of carbon dioxide (CO_2) with water (H_2O) to form carbonic acid (H_2CO_3). The carbonic acid then dissociates into hydrogen and bicarbonate ions. This system acts as a **buffer** in reactions involving hemoglobin and maintains the pH of body fluids at values between 7.35 and 7.45. The basic process looks like this:

$$CO_2 + H_2O \rightleftharpoons H_2CO_3 \rightleftharpoons H^+ + HCO_3^-$$

The proportion of a material that ionizes is called its **degree of dissociation**. Not all substances ionize completely when dissolved in a solvent. It is beyond the intended scope of this book to go into detail on determining the theoretical degree of dissociation of various substances. In addition, extensive tables of accurate values already exist for most common laboratory chemicals.

The degree of dissociation may depend upon a number of factors, such as substance concentration, other substances in the solution, temperature, etc. Formulas that require the use of a substance's degree of dissociation will either use **K** to stand for this value or, in many situations, **pK**. **pK = -log K**. This form is used for compatibility with the pH values that are often in the same formulas.

A commonly used formula is the **Henderson-Hasselbalch relationship**. It is used in pH calculations involving bicarbonate and carbon dioxide concentrations. It says:

$$pH = pK + \log \frac{[HCO_3^-]}{[CO_2]}$$

4.9 BUFFER SOLUTIONS

Buffers act to maintain pH values at or near certain values. Buffer systems are vital to living organisms and in many laboratory procedures. As was mentioned in the previous section, the fluids of the human body must be maintained within narrow pH ranges to properly function. Without properly functioning buffer systems, life would not be possible.

Buffers are made by adding **a weak acid and its salt** to a solution. The acid and salt must be carefully chosen so as to have a **common ion**. The effect of the common ion is to retard the ionization of the weak acid. This will cause the buffer system to resist any change in pH if other acids or bases are added to the solution.

This **common ion effect** will cause the weak acid to dissociate to a lesser degree than the acid would if it were in the solution without the buffer. In a solution of a weak acid and its salt, the salt will usually dissociate completely and the weak acid only slightly. Most of the common ion that is in the solution will come from the salt. This will cause more of the weak acid to remain un-dissociated than would be the case if the acid were in the solution without its salt.

Suppose that we make a buffer using acetic acid (CH_3COOH) and its salt, sodium acetate ($C_2H_3NaO_2$). The acetic acid will slightly dissociate producing some H^+ ions and some $C_2H_3O_2^-$ (acetate) ions. The sodium acetate will dissociate strongly to produce Na^+ ions and $C_2H_3O_2^-$ (acetate) ions. Thus the weak acetic acid and the sodium acetate produce a common ion, acetate ($C_2H_3O_2^-$).

If a strong acid is added to this buffer, it will try to lower the pH. However, the common ion effect will cause many of the H^+ ions from the strong acid to combine with the acetate ions from the salt to form undissociated acetic acid. This process will "gobble up" many of these excess H^+ ions and thus resist (or prevent) a drop in the pH value of the solution.

NOTES

If a strong base is added to this buffer solution it will ionize, producing many excess OH$^-$ ions and try to raise the pH value. However, due to the common ion effect, these excess OH$^-$ ions will combine with the H$^+$ ions from the acetic acid and form water (H$_2$O). This process will "gobble up" the OH$^-$ ions and thus resist any change in the pH value.

The Henderson-Hasselbalch equation is used to do the calculations necessary to make buffer solutions in the lab. Since the relative concentrations of the weak acid and its salt are the important factors, the equation can be re-written as follows:

$$pH = pK + \log \frac{[SALT]}{[ACID]}$$

Example 4.15: Prepare 1 L of acetate buffer that will be 0.2 M and will buffer at a pH of 6.0.

Let's make this buffer using acetic acid, CH$_3$COOH, and a salt that has a common ion, like sodium acetate, C$_2$H$_3$NaO$_2$. The question to be answered is, "How much of each of these compounds are needed?" To use the Henderson-Hasselbalch equation, the pK of the weak acetic acid must be found. As stated previously, this value can be obtained from tables of ionization constants. The pK of acetic acid is 4.75. Now substitute the known values into the equation as follows:

$$6.0 = 4.75 + \log \frac{[SALT]}{[ACID]}$$

$$\log \frac{[SALT]}{[ACID]} = 6.0 - 4.75 = 1.25$$

At this point in our calculation we need to find the antilog of the [SALT] to [ACID] ratio.

$$\log^{-1} 1.25 = 17.8$$

This value, 17.8, is the ratio of the moles per liter of salt and acid in the desired buffer solution.

$$\frac{\text{mol/L salt}}{\text{mol/L acid}} = 17.8$$

Any ratio of salt to acid that yields this ratio may be used. One simple ratio would be 17.8 M salt and 1 M acid. Using these two chosen values, set up a proportion that also contains the desired concentration of 0.2 M as follows:

$$\frac{18.8 \text{ mol/L total}}{1 \text{ mol/L acid}} = \frac{0.2 \text{ mol/L desired total}}{x}$$

$$18.8x = 0.2$$

$$x = 0.011 \text{ mol/L acid}$$

Thus out of the total moles per liter that are needed, 0.011 moles will be acid.

$$\text{mol/L acid} + \text{mol/L salt} = \text{total mol/L}$$

$$0.011 \text{ mol/L acid} + x \text{ mol/L salt} = 0.2 \text{ mol/L total}$$

$$x = 0.189 \text{ mol/L salt}$$

To make the required buffer, the acid and salt need to be measured out in some convenient way. One way is to convert the molarities into the equivalent grams per liter. To do this remember that the molecular weights must be determined first. As this procedure was covered earlier in this book, the values will just be listed here. The molecular weight of acetic acid is 60 g and that of sodium acetate is 82 g.

NOTES

$$\text{(molecular weight acid)(M)} \quad = \quad \text{g/L}$$

$$\text{(60 g)(0.011)} \quad = \quad 0.66 \text{ g/L acid}$$

and

$$\text{(molecular weight salt)(M)} \quad = \quad \text{g/L}$$

$$\text{(82 g)(0.189)} \quad = \quad 15.498 \text{ g/L salt}$$

Now the buffer may be made. To make one liter of the desired buffer, weigh out 0.66 g of acetic acid and 15.498 g of sodium acetate. Dilute up to 1000 ml (1L) and the result will be one liter of a 0.2 M acetate buffer that will buffer at a pH of 6.0. This "recipe" may also be written in a compact form as shown earlier in this book.

0.66 g acetic acid + 15.498 g sodium acetate ⇧ 1000ml ⇨ 1000 ml of 0.2 M acetate buffer, pH = 6.0

Practice Problem Set 4.9:

1. Calculate the pH of a buffer having 0.4 M sodium carbonate and 0.5 M carbonic acid. Assume that the pK of the carbonic acid is 6.10.

2. Calculate the pH of a buffer having 0.085 M sodium acetate and 0.015 M acetic acid with pK = 4.75.

3. In a certain buffering solution the concentration of the salt and acid are equal. What is the pH of this solution?

4. The buffer capacity of a buffer is greatest when pH =_____.

5. How would you make an acetate buffer with a 0.6 N concentration that will buffer at a pH of 7.1?

NOTES

NOTES

CHAPTER SUMMARY

KEY TERMS TO REMEMBER

logarithm	common log	pK
exponent	natural log	buffer
exponential form	antilog	dissociate
logarithmic form	pH	ionize
Henderson-Hasselbalch	pOH	concentration
common ion effect	acid, base and	degree of
	salt relationships	dissociation

FORMULAS TO REMEMBER

You should know how to use each of the following formulas as shown in this chapter.

Exponential Equation Form:	$b^x = y$
Logarithmic Equation Form:	$\log_b y = x$
Common Logarithm Abbreviation:	$\log_{10} = \log$
Natural Logarithm Abbreviation:	$\log_e = \ln$
Antilog Form:	$\log^{-1} x$ or $\ln^{-1} x$

Concentration and
   Ionization Formulas:

$$[H^+] \times [OH^-] = 1 \times 10^{-14}$$

$$N \times \% \text{ ionization} = [H^+]$$

$$pH + pOH = 14$$

$$pH = -\log [H^+]$$

$$pOH = -\log [OH^-]$$

Henderson-Hasselbalch Relationship:

$$pH = pK + \log \frac{[salt]}{[acid]}$$

CHAPTER REVIEW PROBLEMS

1. Find each of the following:

   (a) $\log 20$ (b) $\ln 20$ (c) $\log^{-1} 2.4857$ (d) $\log (-4)$

2. Solve each of the following for x:

   (a) $\log_x 81 = 2$ (b) $\log 0.01 = x$ (c) $\log_5 x = -1$

3. What is the pH of a solution where $[H^+] = 4.2 \times 10^{-5}$?

4. What is the $[OH^-]$ of the solution in number 3 above?

5. If a certain solution has a pOH = 5.2, what is its pH? Is this solution acidic or basic (alkaline)?

6. Find the concentration of hydrogen ions in a bottle of vinegar if its pH = 5.75.

7. A 0.5 N acid solution is only 75% ionized. Calculate each of the following values for this solution:

   (a) $[H^+]$ (b) $[OH^-]$ (c) pH   (d) pOH

8. What is the pH of a bicarbonate buffer having 0.25 M sodium carbonate and 0.075 M carbonic acid? (pK = 6.10)

9. How would you make 200 ml of NaOH solution so that the pH would be 12?

10. How would you prepare 250 ml of an acetate buffer which would buffer at pH = 7.4 and be 0.75 N?

NOTES

SUGGESTED LABORATORY EXERCISES

Note: If this is used by your instructor as an actual laboratory procedure, then more detailed instructions may be needed. It is assumed that you have had one or more courses in chemistry and laboratory procedures prior to this time. Thus, detailed lists of necessary equipment, etc., are not furnished here.

LABORATORY EXERCISE 1: pH OF SOLUTIONS

A. Prepare 500 ml of NaOH solution so that the pH = 11.5.
B. Prepare 500 ml of HCl solution so that the pH = 6.0.

Directions:
1. Calculate, using procedures learned in this chapter, the amount of NaOH necessary to make the required solution.

2. Measure out the NaOH as calculated and dilute up to 500 ml.

3. Measure the pH of the solution you have just made.

4. Compare the pH of the actual solution with what was desired (pH = 11.5). How close is the actual pH to 11.5? If it is not exactly 11.5, why not?

5. Repeat the above using HCl.

LABORATORY EXERCISE 2: BUFFER SOLUTIONS

A. Add an acid to buffer solutions to observe pH changes.

B. Add a base to buffer solutions to observe pH changes.

Directions:

1. Place 5 ml of each of the following in separate test tubes (do two of each and separate them into two sets): distilled water, 0.1 M $NaHCO_3$, 0.1 M NaH_2PO_4, a carbonate buffer (like 0.1 M Na_2CO_3 with 0.1 M $NaHCO_3$), and a phosphate buffer (like 0.1 M NaH_2PO_4 with 0.1 M Na_2HPO_4.) (You should now have ten test tubes in two separate groups of five each.)

2. Measure and record the pH of each test tube.

3. Add one drop of a weak acid like 0.1 M H_3PO_4 (or a specific number of ml as determined by your instructor) to each test tube.

4. Measure and record the pH of each test tube again.

5. Which solution had the largest change in pH? Which had the smallest?

6. Write the equation for the reaction between the acid and one of the buffers used.

7. Take the second set of five test tubes and add one drop of 0.1 M NaOH to each.

8. Repeat steps 4 and 5 as above.

9. Write the equation for the reaction between the base and one of the buffers used.

LABORATORY EXERCISE 3: TESTING COMMERCIAL ANTACID TABLETS

The manufacturers of several commercially available antacid tablets, like Alka Seltzer, Rolaids, etc., claim that their products will consume many times the tablet's weight in excess stomach acid. In this lab these claims will be tested.

✎ **Note:** This is a **titration** procedure. If the techniques of titration have not yet been covered in a previous chemistry class, then your instructor must demonstrate this procedure before you can do it.

Directions:

1. Your lab instructor will choose the antacid brand that you will test. Crush and weigh one tablet. The measurement needs to be to the nearest 0.1 g or better.

2. Fill the buret to be used in the titration with 0.1 M NaOH solution. Be sure there are no bubbles in the tip of the buret.

3. Carefully dissolve the crushed tablet in exactly 100 ml of 0.1 M HCl in an appropriate container.

4. Add 2 drops of bromphenol blue indicator and titrate with the 0.1 M NaOH until the solution turns from yellow to just barely blue.

5. CALCULATIONS:
   If you used the proportions recommended, then the volume of HCl consumed equals 100 ml minus the volume of NaOH used. If it is assumed that 1 ml of 0.1 M HCl weighs 1 g, then the grams of HCl consumed equals the number of grams of HCl consumed. The weight of acid consumed by each gram of antacid tablet is found as follows:

$$\frac{\text{weight of HCl consumed}}{\text{weight of tablet}}$$

6. Does the weight of HCl consumed come close to that claimed by the tablet's manufacturer?

7. If time permits, repeat with a second tablet. Testing just one tablet will not yield the most accurate results. Your instructor may wish to look at the average number of grams of HCl consumed for all tablets tested in the lab class.

NOTES

NOTES

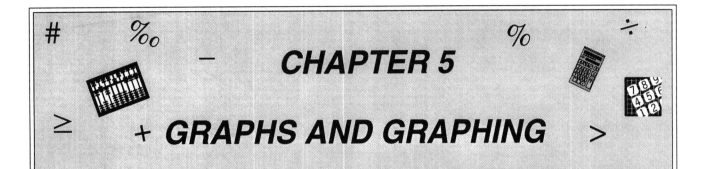

In This Chapter:

5.1 Constructing Graphs

5.2 Interpreting Graphs

5.3 Semi-Log Graphs

5.4 Applications

Chapter Summary

Chapter Review Problems

Suggested Laboratory Exercise

Graphs are used to show how one thing depends upon another. Discovering and understanding relationships between various quantities is common to all of the sciences and important in a laboratory. A graph can be thought of as a "snapshot" of the information that has been gained in a laboratory procedure. A good graph should be intelligible without any additional explanatory information necessary. A well thought out graph will be complete in and of itself.

NOTES

5.1 CONSTRUCTING GRAPHS

Let's assume that you have collected some data in a laboratory procedure and are preparing to graph the information. The first step is to plan the axes of the proposed graph. You will remember from your basic algebra course that a standard graph has two **axes**. One axis is horizontal and is usually called the x-axis. The other is a vertical axis called the y-axis.

In most laboratory procedures, the value of one quantity will depend upon another. For example, the pH of a solution depends upon the amount of acid (or base) present. When planning the axes, the **independent variable** is placed on the **horizontal axis (x-axis)**. The **dependent variable** is placed on the **vertical axis (y-axis)**. The decision as to which variable is the independent one is usually fairly easy to determine. The quantity over which you as the laboratory technician have the most control is usually the independent variable. The other quantity that will change as a result of your manipulation of the independent quantity is the dependent variable. Often you will be asked to do a graph of some quantity versus something else. When stated this way, the quantity mentioned first is the dependent variable and goes on the vertical axis. The quantity that follows the 'versus' is the independent variable and will be placed on the horizontal axis.

Suppose that you wish to add some acid to a solution a little at a time and measure the pH of the solution after each addition. Since you have control over the amount of acid added each time, the amount of acid added will be the independent variable in this situation. The pH depends upon the amount of acid that is added. Thus, the pH measured will be the dependent variable in this hypothetical situation. If a graph of this experiment were to be done, pH values would be placed on the vertical axis and amounts of acid on the horizontal axis. In other words, this would be a graph of pH versus the amount of acid added.

What follows are some brief suggestions to follow that will help to make your graphs easier to construct and read.

1. Your graph should use all of the available space. If you use an 8" by 10" sheet of graph paper, then do an 8" by 10" graph. Don't use just the corner of a large sheet. If the graph needs to be small, then cut down the size of the sheet of graph paper used.

2. It is often good to darken the actual horizontal and vertical axis lines so that they clearly stand out. You do not have to use the outside lines of the graph paper as the x- and y-axis lines. Often there is not enough room for labels and titles along the edges. If this is the case, then choose a line away from the edge as the axis line.

3. When marking the scale along the x- and y-axes, make short lines perpendicular to the axes at points where you plan to label them with numbers. You should not number each line on a graph as it generally makes the scale too crowded. Perhaps numbering every other mark or every fifth or tenth mark would be sufficient. However you choose to mark the scale, be sure the markings and numbers are evenly spaced along both axes.

4. Be sure that you know how much each space represents on each axis. The two axes do not have to be the same scale. Most often the two axes represent two entirely different quantities and cannot be scaled the same. Try to choose scales so that the entire graph is approximately square.

5. Now that the scales have been chosen and marked, be sure to label each axis with the name of the quantity it represents and the units used on the scale.

6. Once you start plotting points on the graph be sure that they are dark enough and big enough to be easily seen. Drawing a small circle around each plotted point is one way of making it stand out. It is also permissible to use little x's for the points instead of dots. In more advanced graphs it is customary to show the probable uncertainty of data points by the size of the arms of a cross. This will be explained in a later chapter on statistics.

7. Once all points have been plotted, it is time to draw a line through them. If the points appear to lie in a straight line (or nearly so) draw a straight line that goes through as many of the plotted points as possible. As a rule of thumb, approximately

NOTES

NOTES

the same number of <u>unconnected</u> points should lie on each side of the line. Do not connect the dots with a meandering point-to-point line unless specifically instructed to do so. (See Figures #1 and #3 on the next page.)

It is possible to calculate the position (or equation) of such a line by performing a statistical analysis of the data points. This statistical method, called regression analysis, is beyond the scope of this text. In most cases, the kinds of graphs that you will construct do not need to be this precise. If there are situations where great precision is required, computer assisted calculations can be easily done with simple statistical programs available in most well equipped labs.

8. If the points do not lie in a straight line, draw a smooth curve that goes through as many of the points as possible. Again, approximately the same number of unconnected points should lie on each side of the curve that you draw. (See Figure #2 on the next page.)

There will almost always be some scattering of points. This will be due to the inevitable uncertainty of measurements made in the lab setting. This scattering will sometimes make it hard for you to decide what the trend of the data is.

9. Be careful not to conceal any points when you draw your line. If a single point seems to be an extreme distance from your line, double check your data for that point. If it is correct, then leave it on your graph but ignore it in placing your line.

10. Remember, not all graphs start or end in the lower left hand corner of the graph (the [0,0] point). Ask yourself if the dependent quantity is zero at the same time that the independent quantity is zero.

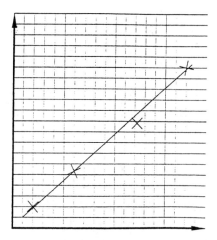

Figure #1

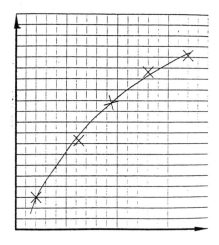

Figure #2

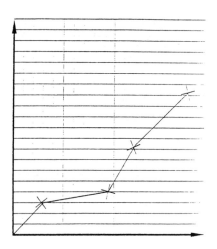

Figure #3

NOTES

NOTES

5.2 INTERPRETING GRAPHS

The shape of a graph can tell you a lot about the relationship between the variables represented on the graph. Below you will find each of the most common possible relationships between the dependent variable (plotted on the y-axis) and the independent variable (plotted on the x-axis). Both the English and algebraic interpretations are given.

CASE A: A straight line that is parallel to the x-axis (Figure #4):

ENGLISH: The dependent variable (y value) is constant, that is, it remains the same for all values of the independent variable (x value). The **slope** of such a line is zero.

ALGEBRA: $y = k$

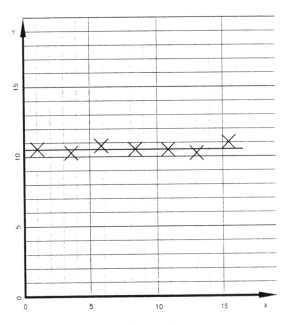

Figure #4

CASE B: A straight line that climbs from left to right (Figure #5):

ENGLISH: The dependent variable (y value) is **directly proportional** to the independent variable (x value). Remember, in a direct proportion, the variables change in the same direction. This means that if x increases, so does y, though not necessarily by the same amount. The slope of this line will be positive.

ALGEBRA: y = kx

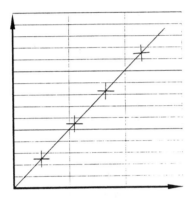

Figure #5

CASE C: A straight line that slopes downward from left to right (Figure #6):

ENGLISH: The dependent variable is **inversely proportional** to the dependent variable. That is, as the x value increases, the y value decreases though not necessarily by the same amount. The slope of this line will be negative.

ALGEBRA: y = k/x

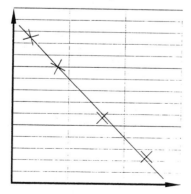

Figure #6

NOTES

CASE D: An upwardly concave smooth curve (Figure #7):

ENGLISH: The dependent variable (y value) is directly proportional to some power of the independent variable (x value).

ALGEBRA: $y = kx^n$

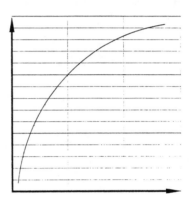

Figure #7

CASE E: A downwardly concave smooth curve (Figure #8):

ENGLISH: The dependent variable is inversely proportional to some power of the independent variable.

ALGEBRA: $y = k/x^n$

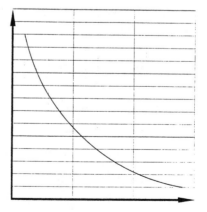

Figure #8

CASE F: A special case where a square root or other root is involved (Figures #9a and #9b):

ENGLISH: The dependent variable is directly proportional to some root of the independent variable (Figure #9a) or, the dependent variable is inversely proportional to some root of the independent variable (Figure #9b).

ALGEBRA: $y = k\sqrt{x}$ (Figure #9a)   or $y = k/\sqrt{x}$ (Figure #9b)

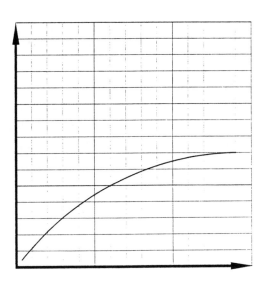

Figure #9a

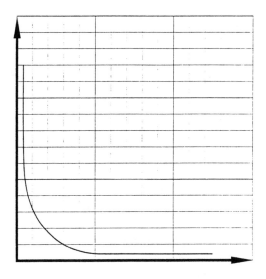

Figure #9b

NOTES

NOTES

OTHER CASES: Graphs of exponential or logarithmic relationships have their own special characteristics. These will be discussed later.

OTHER TERMS: There are several other commonly used terms related to graphs. They are listed here with their definitions. It is assumed that these topics were previously studied by the student in a basic algebra course. No detail or examples are given here.

Slope: Denoted by the letter 'm', it is the change in y divided by the corresponding change in x. Algebraically: $m = \triangle y / \triangle x$.

Extrapolation: The extending of a graph beyond known data points.

Intercepts: The x-intercept is the point at which the line (or curve) crosses the x-axis. At the x-intercept point the value of the y coordinate is zero, (x,0). The y-intercept is the point at which the line crosses the y-axis. At this point the value of the x-coordinate will be zero, (0,y).

Practice Problem Set 5.2:

1. Graph the following set of points. Be sure to follow the directions given in section 5.1 of this chapter. After completing this graph, specify the x- and y-intercept points. Extrapolate the line and determine the value of the y-coordinate when x = 15. Which of the cases listed in this section of Chapter 5 most nearly fits this graph?

x	1	3	7	10	15
y	2	4	8	11	?

x-intercept = (,)
y-intercept = (,)

Interpret the relationship between x and y for this graph.

2. The pressure, P, of a fixed volume of gas (measured in centimeters of mercury) and the temperature, T, (measured in degrees Celsius) are related by the equation $P = (T/4) + 80$.
   (a) Find P when T = 40.
   (b) Find T when P = 100.
   (c) Graph this equation for $40 \leq T \leq 80$.
   (d) What are the x- and y-intercepts of this equation?

3. Graph the following set of data. Which case of those listed in this section of the chapter does this set of data most nearly fit?

x	1/4	1/2	1	2	4
y	-2	-1	0	1	2

4. Graph $y = \log x$ for values of x between 0.1 and 10. What are the x- and y-intercepts of this graph? Which case does it fit?

NOTES

5. An analysis of the concentration of calcium (measured in µg/ml) was made by measuring the absorbance of several known concentrations. Graph the concentration versus the absorbance for the following. Interpret the graph by relating it to the cases listed in this chapter. What would be the approximate concentration of a sample with an absorption of 0.678? Remember, graphs with all decimal values are more difficult to scale and, thus, less accurate than those that are based on whole numbers.

concentration, µg/ml	2.00	4.20	6.01	8.01	10.01	?
absorption	.154	.420	.619	.796	1.0	.678

6. Re-graph the data in problem #5 above, but this time use the percent of transmission value instead of absorption (data listed below). What is the difference in the shape of this graph as compared to the graph you did in #5? What would the percent of transmission be if the concentration was 6.9 µg/ml?

concentration, µg/ml	2.00	4.20	6.01	8.01	10.01	6.9
percent transmission	70%	38%	24%	16%	10%	??

5.3 SEMI-LOG GRAPHS

The graphs we have discussed so far have been concerned with linear and nonlinear functions sketched on rectangular graph paper. The ordinary or rectangular coordinate graph paper has equal spacing on both axes. There are a variety of other types of graph paper available for special purposes. Here we shall look at **semi-logarithmic (semi-log) graph paper**. Semi-log paper (where "semi" means "half") has two different spacings on one graph sheet. One scale is evenly spaced as on rectangular paper, and the other is nonlinear (logarithmic). A point plotted on this paper is a plot of (x , log y) rather than simply (x , y). Figure 10 is a piece of semi-log paper showing three cycles on the logarithmic (vertical) axis.

First let's look at the design and use of semi-log graph paper. The rulings on the vertical axis in Figure 10 are not equally spaced. The rulings are spaced at distances equal to the logarithms of the numbers one through ten. The horizontal axis has rulings that are equally spaced. Note that the lowest number on the logarithmic scale is <u>not</u> zero. Remember from the chapter on logarithms that the logarithm of zero is not defined.

On the vertical axis (the logarithmic scale) of the semi-log graph paper in Figure 10, note that there is a series of sets of numbers 1 through 10. Each set is called a **cycle**. As many cycles as needed may be stacked on top of each other. In Figure 10, three such cycles are shown. Thus, the paper is called three-cycle semi-log graph paper. The number of cycles required to do a particular logarithmic graph is determined by the range of the numbers to be plotted. Figure 11 shows semi-log graph papers with various numbers of cycles.

Numbering the logarithmic scale:

In general, each cycle is numbered so that it is ten times the previous cycle. This is true for graphs involving base ten logs. This means that, on the three-cycle paper shown in Figure 10, if the lowest scale is 1 through 10 in steps of 1 each, the second cycle will be 10 through 100 in steps of 10, and the third cycle will be 100 through 1000 in steps of 100.

NOTES

Any convenient starting point may be chosen. The lowest number on the logarithmic scale does not have to be 1, but may be any power of 10. For example, the scale may begin with 1 and count by ones, begin with 1000 and count by thousands, or begin with .1 and count by tenths, etc. Just be sure that the lowest scale includes the lowest known data point and the upper most cycle includes the highest.

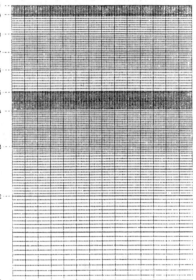

Figure #10
One-Cycle Semi-Log Graph Paper

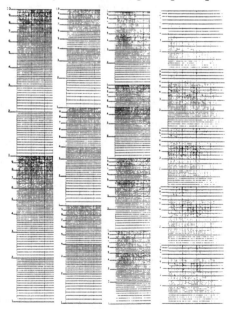

Figure #11
Various Cycles of Semi-Log Graph Paper

| two-cycle semi-log | three-cycle semi-log | four-cycle semi-log | five-cycle semi-log |

Example 5.1:

Graph the following set of data:

x	1	3	5	6	7	9	10	12
y	5000	3000	1000	500	100	60	50	20

First note that there is a very wide range of values for 'y.' This will make doing a graph on ordinary graph paper very difficult. We will do this graph on semi-log graph paper. The y-axis will be the logarithmic axis and represent the numbers with the road range. The x-axis will represent the numbers with the smaller range.

Next we must determine how many cycles we may need to do the graph. Note that the values of 'y' have values in the 10's, 100's and 1000's. That means three cycles are needed. We will number the horizontal scale (the x-axis) equally from 0 (or 1) through about 15 or so, just so that 12 is included. Then we will number the three cycles on the vertical scale (y-axis) 10-100, 100-1000 and 1000-10,000.

Finally plot points. The result is shown in Figure 12.

In addition to making cumbersome sets of numbers a little easier to graph, log and semi-log graph papers make graphing of power functions and exponential functions less troublesome.

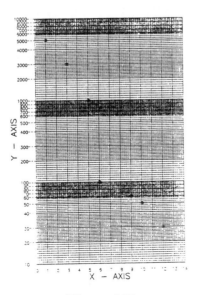

Figure #12
Example 5.1

NOTES

Practice Problem Set 5.3:

Tell which kind of graph paper (rectangular or semi-log) should be used so that the resulting graph would be a straight line (#1-5).

1. $y = 2e^x$ 3. $y = e^{-2}$ 5. $x + y = 10$

2. $y = e^2$ 4. $y = e^{-2x}$

Graph each of the following equations on semi-log graph paper.

6. $y = 2^x$ 8. $y = 2^{-x}$ 10. $y = 5(3^x)$

7. $y = 10^x$ 9. $y = e^{2x}$

11. Graph the following set of data on the appropriate graph paper.

x	0	1	5	12	20	30
y	500	540	735	1260	2330	5030

5.4 APPLICATIONS

One major use of graphs in the laboratory is as a reference for tests that are to be performed. If a test is to be performed to determine the concentration of a certain substance in an unknown solution, plotting a **standard curve** for comparison is very useful, especially if repeated tests are to be done for various unknown concentrations of the same substance.

In the clinical chemistry laboratory, many procedures are performed by **spectrophotometry**. Spectrophotometry takes advantage of the property of colored solutions to absorb light of specific wavelengths. In a **spectrophotometer**, a colored liquid is placed in a transparent holder called a **cuvette**. Light of an appropriate wavelength is then passed through the cuvette and its liquid contents. Some of the light will be absorbed by the liquid and some will pass through. This whole process may also be called **colorimetry** in other texts, and the device may be called a **colorimeter**.

Various measurements are made by the spectrophotometer. The intensity of the light that strikes the sample is measured. In formulas below, the intensity of this incident light is I_o. The intensity of the light that is able to pass through the sample is also measured. The intensity of the light that is transmitted through the sample will be denoted as I_t. A simple proportion is then set up to compare the original intensity, I_o, with the intensity of the light transmitted through the sample, I_t, and the result is called the **percent transmission (%T)**.

$$\frac{I_t}{I_o} \times 100\% = \%T$$

A value of I_o is usually obtained by using either water or a reagent blank in the cuvette. The value of %T for I_o is thus the percent of light transmitted with no concentration of the substance in question.

Next, various known concentrations of the substance in question are made and the %T values found with the spectrophotometer. As the concentration is increased, the color of the substance (or coloring agent used) will deepen and less and less light will be transmitted through the cuvette. Thus, the value of %T will go down.

The relationship between concentration and percent transmittance is not linear. If a graph of these known values is to be done so that a straight line results, **semi-log graph paper** must be used. %T numbers are plotted on the logarithmic scale and concentrations on the rectangular scale.

Another quantity may also be calculated. The amount of light that is absorbed by the colored solution in the cuvette is called **absorbance (A) or optical density (OD)**. Of course, the %T and OD numbers are closely related. Absorbance or optical density may be calculated as follows:

$$A = OD = \log \frac{1}{T} \quad \text{or} \quad A = OD = -\log T$$

Table VI of the Appendix has an extensive list of equivalent absorbance/percent transmission values that can be used.

If absorbance values are used instead of %T's and a graph is then plotted vs. substance concentration, a straight line will result if standard rectangular graph paper is used instead of semi-log paper.

Thus, to plot %T vs. substance concentration, use semi-log paper. To plot OD vs. substance concentration, use rectangular paper.

The relationship between absorbance (A) or optical density (OD), and substance concentration can be expressed in an equation known as **Beer's Law**:

$$A = abC$$

or

$$OD = abC$$

Beer's Law says that the absorbance or optical density of a substance depends upon its concentration, C, the length of the path that the light follows through the cuvette in the spectrophotometer, b, and another constant called an absorptivity coefficient, a.

The length of the path through the cuvette, b, in the Beer's Law equation will be a constant value for a particular spectrophotometer. The **absorptivity coefficient** is also a constant. This means that **absorbance or optical density is directly proportional to substance concentration**.

In normal spectrophotometer procedures, the values of the absorbance, A or OD, and/or percent transmission, %T, of a series of standards of known concentration are found. These values are then used to plot a graph known as a **standard curve**. It is called a standard "curve" even though the graphs made are straight lines if plotted on the proper type of graph paper. As mentioned above:

1. plot **%T vs. concentration** on **semi-log** graph paper;
2. plot **A vs. concentration** on **regular** graph paper.

A standard curve is used as a time saving device for determining the unknown concentrations of substances in everyday laboratory measurements. The measured absorbance or percent transmission of an unknown concentration of a given substance may be quickly compared to the standard curve for that substance and the concentration may then be read off of the graph with relative ease and some accuracy.

Of course, it is also possible to calculate the value of an unknown concentration by remembering that absorbance and substance concentration are directly related. Let's first choose some symbols to use and define them:

A_u = the absorbance of the unknown as measured in the lab

A_s = the absorbance of a known concentration from the standard curve for the substance in question

C_u = the concentration of the unknown substance
C_s = the concentration from the standard curve that goes with the chosen value of A_s.

Now we can set up an equation based on the direct proportion that exists between A and C as follows:

$$\frac{A_u}{A_s} = \frac{C_u}{C_s}$$

If the equation above is then rearranged so that it is easily solved for the unknown concentration, the following working equation is obtained:

$$C_u = C_s \left(\frac{A_u}{A_s} \right)$$

NOTES

NOTES

Example 5.2:

The concentration of NaCl in serum is to be determined for a single sample. To find this unknown concentration, a standard curve will be plotted using %T values vs known NaCl concentrations in serum.

STEP 1: Find the percent transmission for a **reagent blank, also called a reference blank**, in the spectrophotometer. A reagent blank is made by placing pure serum (saline) and any reagents that will be used in a cuvette and placing it in the spectrophotometer. With the reagent blank in the machine, reset the readings to 100%T (or 0 absorbance). This means that any observed changes in %T seen in future serum samples containing NaCl will be due to the NaCl present.

STEP 2: Next make a series of known concentrations of NaCl in serum and measure the %T value for each. The following table shows a hypothetical set of such values:

NaCl conc. X 10^{-4} M	Percent T
2.00	43.9
3.50	33.7
5.00	24.8
7.50	15.4

STEP 3: Now plot the graph of %T values vs the molar concentration. Figure #13 on the next page shows the result of this step. Remember, use single cycle semi-log paper for this graph.

STEP 4: Now measure the %T of the unknown. Let's suppose that this was done and the value obtained was 38.4%. The value of the molar concentration in the unknown sample may be read directly from the standard curve as shown in Figure #14. (2.6 X 10^{-4} M)

Using the standard curve in Figure #13, find the concentration of a sample with %T = 10%. (9.8 X 10^{-4} M)

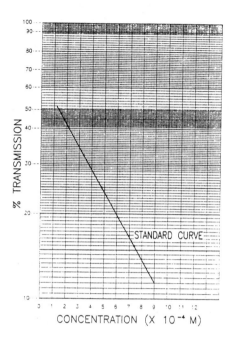

Figure #13
Step 3 of Example 5.2

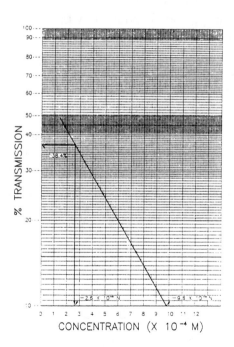

Figure #14
Step 4 of Example 5.2

NOTES

Practice Problem Set 5.4:

1. An analysis of known concentrations of calcium (measured in µg/ml) is made and the results are shown in the following table of data:

Conc. of Ca in µg/ml	%T
1.8	70.0
4.4	37.5
6.3	24.0
8.0	16.0
10.0	10.0

(a) Plot a standard curve for this data. (b) If a sample is measured and shows a %T of 21%, what is the calcium concentration indicated on your standard curve? (c) Calculate the calcium concentration using the proper equation from this section of the chapter. (d) What is the percent difference between the calcium concentration estimated by the graph as compared to the calculated value? (e) Repeat parts (b), (c) and (d) if the %T of another unknown calcium concentration is 17%.

2. Several standard iron (II) solutions were prepared in a solution that contained an excess of 1,10 phenanthroline. The absorbance of each iron (II) - 1,10 phenanthroline (complex) solution was measured in a 1.00 cm cell at a wavelength of 508 nm in a spectrophotometer. The concentrations and corresponding absorbance values measured are tabulated below. Determine, graphically, the concentration of a sample of the same solution if the measured absorbance is 0.482.

Concentration X 10^{-5} M	Absorbance Measured
2.8	0.201
5.6	0.403
8.4	0.598
11.2	0.808
14.0	1.010

3. The percent transmittance of a series of solutions of a certain organic compound were measured at a wavelength of 254 nm in a cuvette with a path length of 1.00 cm. The data are listed in the table below. (a) What would be the concentration of a sample with absorbance = 0.482? (b) Approximately what should the absorbance be for a sample with a concentration of 6.5×10^{-5} M?

Concentration $\times 10^{-5}$ M	%T
1.25	63.1%
2.50	39.7%
3.75	24.9%
5.00	15.7%
6.25	10.1%

4. Convert each of the given %T values in the following table to the corresponding absorbance value.

%T Value	Absorbance A or OD
70.0%	
45.8%	
30.5%	
19.4%	
1.25%	

5. Convert each of the following absorbancies to the equivalent %T value.

A (OD)	%T
1.523	
0.523	
0.119	
0.073	
2.000	

NOTES

NOTES

CHAPTER SUMMARY

KEY TERMS TO REMEMBER

independent variable   dependent variable
direct proportions   inverse proportions
slope   extrapolation
intercepts   cuvette
spectrophotometry   colorimetry
absorbance   optical density
Beer's Law   percent transmission
standard curve   semi-log graph
reference or reagent blank

FORMULAS TO REMEMBER

You should know how to use each of the following formulas as shown in this chapter.

slope: $m = \Delta y / \Delta x$

percent transmission: $(I_t/I_o) \times 100\% = \%T$

absorbance (or OD): $A = OD = \log(1/T)$
                            $A = OD = -\log T$

Beer's Law: $A = abC$

unknown concentration: $C_u = C_s(A_u/A_s)$

GRAPHING

The only way to become good at graphing is by practicing. You should work all the problems in this chapter so that you can easily create semi-log graphs and, perhaps more importantly, correctly interpret them.

CHAPTER REVIEW PROBLEMS

1. George and Mary filled their gas tank before they drove out of town on vacation. Every once in a while they stopped to buy gas and checked their cumulative mileage. They drove 110 miles and bought 4.3 gallons. They drove on until their mileage totaled 250 miles and bought 4.0 gallons more. They then drove on until they had been a total of 400 miles and bought 6.1 gallons more. (a) Plot a graph of total miles traveled vs total gallons. (b) What was their mileage? (c) What is the slope of the line in the graph?

2. A standard supply of glucose has a concentration of 200 mg/ml stated on its label and, when tested in a spectrophotometer, shows %T = 38%. A glucose sample of unknown concentration is also tested and shows %T = 59%. What is the concentration?

3. A lab technician makes a solution of bilirubin that has a concentration of 150 ml/L. This solution has an optical density of 0.35, as determined on a spectrophotometer. What is the concentration of a similar solution of bilirubin if its optical density is shown to be 0.18?

4. Plot the following data on the proper graph paper. Use the standard curve you have drawn to determine the concentration of a sample that shows %T = 33%.

Concentration X 10^{-5} M	Percent Transmission (%T)
2.8	63
5.6	40
8.4	25
11.2	16
14.0	10

NOTES

5. Graph the following data set on the proper graph paper. Use the standard curve you have drawn to determine the concentration of a sample that has an optical density of 0.56.

Concentration X 10⁻⁵ M	Optical Density
1.25	0.20
2.50	0.40
3.75	0.60
5.00	0.80
6.25	1.00

SUGGESTED LABORATORY EXERCISES

LABORATORY EXERCISE 1: MEASURING PERCENT TRANSMISSION

If you have access to a spectrophotometer, the following may be done. Your instructor can have you prepare and measure the percent transmission (or optical density/absorbance) of a series of known concentrations. Refer to the laboratory exercise in Chapter 2 for more complete instructions. Use this information to construct a standard curve. Then you may be asked to determine the concentration of various samples of unknown concentration provided by your lab instructor using the spectrophotometer and the graph that you have created.

NOTES

NOTES

In This Chapter:

During the past two decades, automated cell counting instruments have become increasingly important in the laboratory. They are used to directly measure RBCs, WBCs and platelets. Hematocrit, MCH and MCHC are then electronically calculated from the data. However, there are still specimens of blood and body fluids that require a manual count. The mathematics of determining a correct manual blood count is presented in this chapter. An understanding of this basic procedure will also aid the student in understanding the results generated by an automated count. Because of the care and instrumentation needed for doing manual blood counts in a clinical laboratory, no laboratory exercise will be included in this chapter.

6.1 INTRODUCTION - MANUAL BLOOD COUNTS

Cell enumeration using a hemacytometer is a widely used method and continues to have a place in most laboratories, including those that are now equipped with electronic cell counters. A good grasp of basic hematologic procedures will serve as a building block for student understanding and for applications of more advanced technology that the student may encounter in a laboratory.

Manual cell counts are done in a hemacytometer counting chamber such as the one illustrated in Figure #1. The Neubauer hemacytometer is used for most blood counts. It contains two chambers separated by an H-shaped moat. Each surface of the chamber contains a square area which is ruled into nine squares of 1 mm² each. The two squares are exactly alike allowing a technologist to dupli-

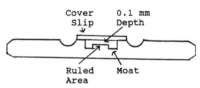

Figure #1

cate the count. A coverslip is supported above this area and is exactly 0.1 mm above the ruled areas. Therefore, when the chamber is filled, the volume of the cell suspension over each square is 0.1 mm³.

The diagram in Figure #2 shows an enlarged view of one of the two ruled squares of the hemacytometer. The four corner primary squares are used for counting white cells. Each corner square has an area of 1.0 mm² and is divided into 16 smaller squares to aid in the counting process. The center primary square is divided into 25 smaller secondary squares. Five of these smaller squares (the four corner ones and the middle one) are used for counting red blood cells. Each of these small secondary squares has an area of 0.04 mm². All 25 secondary squares of the center primary square are used to count platelets.

6.2 DILUTING A BLOOD SAMPLE

In most laboratories, the dilution of a blood sample is done using a prepackaged blood dilution vial such as the Unopette kit by Becton-Dickinson and Company. The vials used for white blood counts contain 1.98 ml of diluent mixture and a capillary pipette with a 20 μL (0.02 ml) capacity. The pipette is filled with blood by capillary action and then mixed with the premeasured diluent resulting in a 1/100 dilution ratio. Dilution ratios are different for red blood counts (1/200) and may vary with the manufacturer. The dilution ratio can be obtained from the information sheet accompanying the premeasured vials.

The dilution of a blood sample may also be done using a cell-diluting pipette. These pipettes are primarily used for measuring body fluids such as cerebral spinal fluid (CSF) and for joint cell fluid counts. The pipettes for red blood cell counts (RBC) and white blood cell counts (WBC) are composed of a stem that is divided into 10 equal parts and a mixing chamber which contains a bead that aids in the mixing of the blood and the diluent. The pipette used for a WBC contains a clear bead while the one used for a RBC contains a red bead.

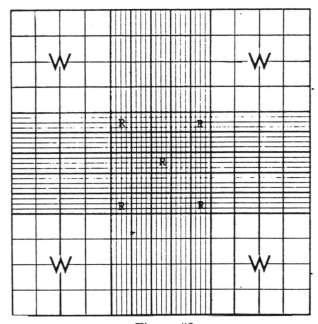

Figure #2

In a WBC pipette, blood is drawn to either the 0.5 or 1.0 mark and the diluent to the 11 mark. This produces 10 volumes of diluted blood in the mixing chamber. One volume of diluent remains in the stem. If the blood is drawn to the 0.5 mark, then the dilution ratio is 0.5/10 or 1/20. If blood is to the 1.0 mark, the dilution is ratio 1/10.

A RBC pipette has a total capacity of 101 volumes. Blood is usually drawn to the 0.5 or 1,0 mark and the diluent to the 101 mark. This produces 100 volumes of diluted blood in the mixing chamber and one volume of diluent in the stem. The resulting dilutions are 0.5/100 (1/200) and 1/100, respectively.

A **dilution factor** will be needed when calculating the number of cells in a blood sample. This factor will be the reciprocal of the dilution done. If a Unopette is used, for example, the dilution factor will be 100 since the original dilution was 0.02 ml/1.98 ml or 1/100. When the dilution factor is multiplied times the number of cells counted in a diluted sample, a number representing the cell count for an undiluted sample results.

6.3 PROCEDURES FOR A WBC COUNT

White blood cells (leukocytes) are counted in the four corner primary squares of the ruled area of the counting chamber. Each primary square has dimensions 1 mm × 1 mm and is divided into 16 smaller squares. Count cells starting in the small square in the upper left corner. Move across the top row of squares and then drop down to the next row and move from right to left. Continue counting in a similar fashion until all small squares have been counted. (See Figure #3.)

Cells that touch the left side or the top of the square should be counted. Cells touching the right side or bottom of the square are not counted. The total cell count for the square in Figure #3 would be 31. The values tabulated from the four primary squares should not vary more than 10 cells. When a larger variation occurs, another dilution should be done for a more accurate reading.

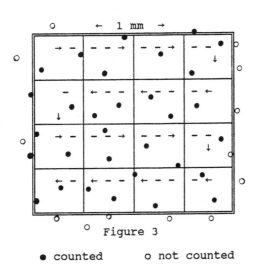

Figure 3

● counted   ○ not counted

Figure #3

White cell counts are reported as number of cells per microliter (μL), number of cells per milliliter (ml), or number of cells per liter (L). Laboratories that have formerly reported WBC in cells/mm^3 are now reporting counts in standard SI units as cells/L. Volume units that are reported in a medical laboratory test may differ from those required in a biotechnology laboratory research project. Therefore, close attention should be given to the units required for a particular procedure. Variations in the volume units are made by adjusting the power of 10 needed to convert from the basic volume unit to the desired unit.

NOTES

The volume of liquid above each large ruled square in the counting chamber (Volume = length × width × height or depth) is 1 mm × 1 mm × 0.1 mm or 0.1 mm^3. Since 1 mm^3 = 1 μL, the volume in the chamber can be expressed as 0.1 μL. Therefore, if a cell count is 6500/mm^3, this count can also be expressed as 6500/μL. If the desired volume unit is milliliters, the cell count/μL should be multiplied by 10^3 since 1 ml = 10^3 μL. If the desired volume unit is liters, the cell count/μL should be multiplied by a factor of 10^6 since 1 L = 10^{6}μL.

Example 6.1: The results of a WBC count are 2500 WBC/mm^3. Give the number that should be reported as:
a) cells/μL   b) cells/ml   c) cells/L

a) 2500 WBC/mm^3 = 2500 WBC/μL

b) 2500 WBC/mm^3 × 10^3 = 2,500,000 or 2.5 × 10^6 WBC/ml

c) 2500 WBC/mm^3 × 10$^{6.}$ = 2,500,000,000 or 2.5 × 10^9 WBC/L

In calculating the number of cells in a blood count, several things must be taken into consideration:

1. How you wish to express the count (cells/mm^3, /ml, or /L).

2. The dilution of blood.

3. The number of squares counted.

The following formulas should be used to calculate the white cell count for a blood sample. The formulas differ in only the power of 10 used to give the desired volume unit for the procedure being done.

```
                CALCULATING A WBC COUNT

Total Cells Counted  ×  Dilution  × 10  =  cells/mm³
Number Squares           Correction
    Counted                  Factor



Total Cells Counted  ×  Dilution  × 10⁴ = cells/ml
Number Squares           Correction
    Counted                  Factor


Total Cells Counted  ×  Dilution  × 10⁷  = cells/L
Number Squares           Correction
    Counted                  Factor
```

$$\frac{\text{Total Cells Counted}}{\text{Number Squares Counted}} \times \text{Dilution Correction Factor} \times 10 = \text{cells/mm}^3$$

$$\frac{\text{Total Cells Counted}}{\text{Number Squares Counted}} \times \text{Dilution Correction Factor} \times 10^4 = \text{cells/ml}$$

$$\frac{\text{Total Cells Counted}}{\text{Number Squares Counted}} \times \text{Dilution Correction Factor} \times 10^7 = \text{cells/L}$$

If white blood cells are counted in the four corner squares, find the total number of cells and divide by four. This is a way of deriving an average number of cells for the count. Remember that standard cell counting convention includes in a count all cells that touch the upper or left boundary lines, but none of those that touch the lower or right boundary lines. Using this method will help avoid counting cells twice resulting in a more accurate result. (The middle of the three lines spaced 2.5 μm apart is considered to be the boundary line.) A duplicate count can be done on the second grid in the hemacytometer to check for consistency.

Example 6.2: Blood is diluted using a Unopette vial. The four primary corner squares are counted with totals as follows: 10 cells, 12 cells, 11 cells, 9 cells. Calculate the number of cells/mm³(μL) in this blood sample.

1. The dilution was 0.02/1.98 or 1/100. Therefore, the dilution correction factor will be the reciprocal of this dilution, or 100.

2. Total cells counted in four squares = 42.

3. Our results are to be reported as cells/mm³ so the following formula should be used:

NOTES

NOTES

$$\frac{\text{Total Cells Counted}}{\text{Number of Squares}} \times \frac{\text{Dilution}}{\text{Correction}} \times 10 = \text{cells/mm}^3$$

Number of Squares   Correction
        Counted   Factor

$$\frac{42}{4} \times 100 \times 10 = 10500 \text{ cells/mm}^3$$

Therefore, the original blood sample contains 10500 white blood cells/mm³ or 10500 WBC/µL.

A second method of calculating direct cell counts involves the calculation of a volume correction factor. The desired volume (1.0 mm³) is divided by the volume used for the count (0.4 mm³ if the four primary corner squares are used). This results in a volume correction factor that is then multiplied times the total number of cells counted and the dilution factor. This product is the number of cells/mm³ for the blood sample.

Number ×	Dilution ×	Volume =	Cells/mm³
of Cells	Correction	Correction	
Counted	Factor	Factor	

Example 6.3: A blood sample is diluted using a Unopette vial. A total of 50 white cells are counted in the four primary corner squares. What WBC should be reported for this sample?

number of cells counted = 50

dilution correction factor = 100

$$\text{volume correction factor} = \frac{\text{desired volume}}{\text{volume used}} = \frac{1.0 \text{ mm}^3}{0.4 \text{ mm}^3} = 2.5$$

Number Cells × Dilution × Volume = cells/mm³
                    Correction   Correction
                    Factor   Factor

$$50 \times 100 \times 2.5 = 12500 \text{ cells/mm}^3$$

6.4 PROCEDURES FOR AN RBC COUNT

In order to count red blood cells (erythrocytes), the small squares inside the larger center square of the grid are used. (See Figure #2.) The number of cells is counted in the same manner as previously explained by counting all cells that touch the upper and left boundary lines. A separate count can be done on the duplicate grid in the hemacytometer to check consistency of results.

The squares that are used for the RBC are 0.2 mm on each side or 0.04 mm^2 in area. Each small square is 1/25 (0.04) the size of the large center square which measures 1 mm^2. Therefore, in the formula a correction for these 25 subdivisions is made. To calculate an RBC use one of the following formulas depending on the volume unit required in reporting results.

CALCULATING AN RBC COUNT

$$\frac{\text{Number Cells Counted}}{\substack{\text{Number Squares} \\ \text{Counted}}} \times 25 \times \substack{\text{Dilution.} \\ \text{Correction} \\ \text{Factor}} \times 10 = \text{Cells/mm}^3$$

$$\frac{\text{Number Cells Counted}}{\substack{\text{Number Squares} \\ \text{Counted}}} \times 25 \times \substack{\text{Dilution} \\ \text{Correction} \\ \text{Factor}} \times 10^4 = \text{Cells/ml}$$

$$\frac{\text{Number Cells Counted}}{\substack{\text{Number Squares} \\ \text{Counted}}} \times 25 \times \substack{\text{Dilution} \\ \text{Correction} \\ \text{Factor}} \times 10^7 = \text{Cells/L}$$

In most situations, five squares (the four corner ones and the central one) are counted when determining the red blood count. When this is done, the formula can be reduced to the following simplified version:

<table>
<tr><td>

NOTES

</td><td>

CALCULATING AN RBC COUNT (five squares counted)

Numbers × 5 ×   Dilution   × 10 = cells/mm³
Cells   Correction
Counted   Factor

</td></tr>
</table>

An alternative method of calculating RBC can be done by determining a volume correction factor using the same procedure that was done for the WBC. The volume correction factor is calculated by dividing the desired volume by the volume used for the count. If five small squares in the center primary square are counted, then the volume used for the count is $5/25 \times 1/10 = .02$ mm³. This number is divided into the desired volume (1.0 mm³) and a volume correction factor is obtained.

Example 6.4: Blood is drawn to the 0.5 mark of a RBC pipette. Cells are counted in the four corner and the center secondary squares. The total number of cells counted is 480. The depth of the counting chamber is 0.1 mm. Calculate the cell count/mm³.

1. Using the formula:

   Blood drawn to 0.5 mark results in 1/200 dilution. Therefore, the dilution correction factor is 200.

   Number × 5 × Dilution   × 10 = cells/mm³
   Cells   Correction
   Counted   Factor

   $480 \times 5 \times 200 \times 10 = x$ cells/mm³

   $4,800,000$ or 4.8×10^6 RBC/mm³ $= x$

2. Using a volume correction factor:

   $$\text{Factor} = \frac{\text{Desired Volume}}{\text{Volume Used}} = \frac{1.00 \text{ mm}^3}{0.02 \text{ mm}^3} = 50$$

   Number Cells   ×   Volume   ×   Dilution   =   RBC/mm³
      Counted   Correction   Correction

   $480 \times 50 \times 200 = 4,800,000 = 4.8 \times 10^6$ cells/mm³

Practice Problem Set 6.4:

1. Give the dilution factors for the blood in a WBC pipette if blood is drawn to:

   a. the 0.5 mark   b. the 1.0 mark

2. Give the dilution factors for the blood in a RBC pipette if blood is drawn to:

   a. the 0.5 mark   b. the 1.0 mark

3. If a manual WBC count results in a count of 6800 cells/µL, what results would be reported per milliliter? per liter?

4. Blood is diluted for a white blood count using a Unopette vial. A total of 150 cells is counted in the four large corner primary squares. Find the WBC count as cells/ml for this blood sample.

5. Blood is drawn to the 0.5 mark on an RBC pipette. The cells in the four corner and center secondary squares are counted and a total cell count of 440 RBCs is obtained. Report the correct cell count/mm^3 for this sample.

6. How many white blood cells are in the corner square shown in the figure at the right.

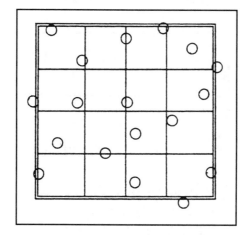

7. A WBC is done using a Unopette vial. The number of cells in each of the four corner squares is counted as follows: 12, 9, 15, and 13. What is the correct cell count/L?

Problem #6

NOTES

6.5 RBC INDICES

There are three RBC indices that are commonly calculated which help define the size and hemoglobin content of the average red blood cell (erythrocyte) in a given blood sample. These indices aid in the classification of anemia.

The three most commonly used RBC indices include the **mean corpuscular volume (MCV), mean corpuscular hemoglobin (MCH),** and **mean corpuscular hemoglobin concentration (MCHC).** The definitions and calculations of these indices are explained in this section.

MEAN CORPUSCULAR VOLUME

The **mean corpuscular volume (MCV)** is the average volume of a red blood cell expressed in μm^3 (also known as cubic microns, μ^3) or in femtoliters (fl). Normal red blood cells have a MCV between 80 and 98 fl.

The following formula will enable you to calculate the MCV. The hematocrit (Hct) is defined to be the proportion of red blood cells in whole blood expressed as a percent.

$$MCV = \frac{Hematocrit\ (\%) \times 10}{RBC\ count\ (in\ millions/\mu L)}$$

MEAN CORPUSCULAR HEMOGLOBIN

The **mean corpuscular hemoglobin (MCH)** is the weight of hemoglobin (Hb) in the average red blood cells of a specimen. The result is given in picograms (pg) (or micromicrograms $\mu\mu g$). The normal MCH in adults is 27 pg to 31 pg. The value will generally be higher in newborns and infants because their MCV is higher than in adults.

The following formula will enable you to calculate the MCH.

$$MCH = \frac{\text{Hemoglobin (g/dl)} \times 10}{\text{RBC count (in millions/}\mu\text{L)}}$$

MEAN CORPUSCULAR HEMOGLOBIN CONCENTRATION

The **mean corpuscular hemoglobin concentration (MCHC)** is the average concentration of hemoglobin in each individual red blood cell given as a percent. It is the percent of hemoglobin in the packed cell volume. Normal values are rounded to tenths place and range from 33% to 38%.

The formula to calculate MCHC is:

$$MCHC = \frac{\text{Hemoglobin (g/dl)} \times 100}{\text{Hematocrit}}$$

The mean corpuscular hemoglobin concentration is the ratio of the mass of the mean corpuscular hemoglobin (MCH) and the mean corpuscular volume (MCV) expressed as a percent. Therefore, any of these values can be calculated from the others if two of the three values are known. The following formulas express this relationship.

$$MCHC = \frac{MCH}{MCV} \times 100$$

$$MCH = 0.01\ MCHC \times MCV$$

$$MCV = \frac{MCH}{0.01\ MCHC}$$

NOTES

NOTES

Example 6.5: You are given the following information.

RBC = 4,500,000; Hb = 14 g; Hct = 41%

Calculate these indices: MCV, MCH, and MCHC.

a. MCV = $\dfrac{\text{Hematocrit (Hct)} \times 10}{\text{RBC count (in millions/}\mu\text{L)}}$

   MCV = $\dfrac{41 \times 10}{4.5}$

   MCV = $\dfrac{410}{4.5}$

   MCV = 91.1 μm^3 or 91.1 fl

b. MCH = $\dfrac{\text{Hemoglobin (in g/dl)} \times 10}{\text{RBC count (in millions/}\mu\text{L)}}$

   MCH = $\dfrac{14 \times 10}{4.5}$

   MCH = $\dfrac{140}{4.5}$

   MCH = 31.1 pg

c. MCHC = $\dfrac{\text{Hemoglobin (in g/dl)} \times 100}{\text{Hematocrit, \%}}$

   MCHC = $\dfrac{14 \times 100}{41}$

   MCHC = $\dfrac{1400}{41}$

   MCHC = 34.1%

Practice Problem Set 6.5:

Calculate the RBC indices - MCV, MCH, MCHC - for each problem using the given information.

1. red blood cell count - 5,500,000
    hemoglobin (Hb) - 15 g%
    hematocrit (Hct) - 50%

2. red blood cell count - 4,300,000
    hemoglobin (Hb) - 11.5 g%
    hematocrit (Hct) - 40%

3. red blood cell count - 2,400,000
    hemoglobin (Hb) - 5 g%
    hematocrit (Hct) - 24%

4. red blood cell count - 3,600,000
    hemoglobin (Hb) - 5.4 g%
    hematocrit (Hct) - 38%

5. red blood cell count - 4,500,000
    hemoglobin (Hb) - 10.4 g%
    hematocrit (Hct) - 32%

NOTES

NOTES

CHAPTER SUMMARY

KEY TERMS TO REMEMBER

hemacytometer   Neubauer ruling
white blood count (WBC)   red blood count (RBC)
dilution correction factor   volume correction factor
mean corpuscular volume (MCV)
mean corpuscular hemoglobin (MVH)
mean corpuscular hemoglobin concentration (MCHC)

FORMULAS TO REMEMBER

WHITE BLOOD COUNT

$$\frac{\text{Total Cells Counted}}{\substack{\text{Number Squares}\\ \text{Counted}}} \times \substack{\text{Dilution}\\ \text{Correction}\\ \text{Factor}} \times 10 = \text{cells/mm}^3$$

$$\substack{\text{Number}\\ \text{of Cells}\\ \text{Counted}} \times \substack{\text{Dilution}\\ \text{Correction}\\ \text{Factor}} \times \substack{\text{Volume}\\ \text{Correction}\\ \text{Factor}} = \text{cells/mm}^3$$

RED BLOOD COUNT

$$\frac{\text{Number Cells Counted}}{\substack{\text{Number Squares}\\ \text{Counted}}} \times 25 \times \substack{\text{Dilution}\\ \text{Correction}\\ \text{Factor}} \times 10 = \text{cells/mm}^3$$

$$\substack{\text{Number Cells}\\ \text{Counted}} \times 5 \times \substack{\text{Dilution}\\ \text{Correction}\\ \text{Factor}} \times 10 = \text{cells/mm}^3$$

$$\text{MCV} = \frac{\text{Hematocrit (\%)} \times 10}{\text{RBC count (in millions/}\mu\text{L)}}$$

$$\text{MCH} = \frac{\text{Hemoglobin (g/dl)} \times 10}{\text{RBC count (in millions/}\mu\text{L)}}$$

$$\text{MCHC} = \frac{\text{Hemoglobin (g/dl)} \times 100}{\text{Hematocrit}}$$

CHAPTER REVIEW PROBLEMS

1. 100 white blood cells were counted in the four 1 mm² corners of the grid of a Neubauer hemacytometer. A 1:20 dilution of the blood sample was done.
   a. Report the results of this WBC as cells/mm³.
   b. Report the results as cells/L.

2. The square at the right is one of the four corner squares used for a WBC. How many cells should be counted for this square if they are distributed as shown in the diagram?

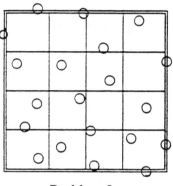

Problem 2

3. Blood is drawn to the 0.5 mark in a RBC diluting pipette. In five small squares of the center in a Neubauer hemacytometer, 235 cells are counted. What is the RBC in cells/μL?

4. Calculate the WBC in cells/μL if blood is diluted using a Unopette vial and a total of 45 WBCs are counted in the four corner primary squares of a Neubauer hemacytometer.

5. Calculate the MCV, MCH and MCHC for the following data:

   a. RBC: 5.0×10^6 cells/μL
      Hemoglobin: 14 g/dl
      Hematocrit: 45%

   b. RBC: 6,350,000 cells/μL
      Hemoglobin: 12g%
      Hematocrit: 41%

6. If 2500 WBC/μL is the count for a blood sample, what numbers would you report if the count is to be given as
   a. cells/ml?   b. cells/L?

NOTES

7. A Unopette vial is used to do a dilution for a red blood count. The resulting dilution ratio is 1/200. A total of 320 cells is counted in the five small squares in the center square of the grid. Give the RBC in cells/μL for this sample.

8. Blood is drawn up in a WBC pipette to the 0.5 mark. The total number of white cells counted in the four corner squares is 78. Give the cell count/ml for this sample.

9. If the MCV is 75.5 μm^3 and the MCH is 22.9 pg, calculate the MCHC as a %.

In This Chapter:

Statistics is looked upon as a difficult subject by most students. Many equate statistics with mathematical slight of hand or deception. For example, Benjamin Disraeli said, "There are three kinds of lies: lies, @#$%&*! lies and statistics." Mark Twain said, "Get the facts first and then you can distort them as much as you please." Perhaps Benjamin Leacock summed up this attitude best when he said, "In earlier times they had no statistics, and so they had to fall back on lies. They did it with lies, we do it with statistics; but it's all the same thing."

In this chapter you will learn what statistics is really all about and how it is a useful tool in the laboratory. We hope that you will find that statistics is an interesting area of mathematics, and one that can yield useful information.

NOTES

7.1 BASIC TOPICS

Statistics is an area of mathematics that deals with collecting, organizing and interpreting data. More specifically, statistics are used to help draw conclusions based on a *limited* amount of information. This process includes data collection, determination of actual attributes or qualities (such as size, color, etc.), making estimates, and constructing hypotheses about probable values.

DESCRIPTIVE VS INFERENTIAL STATISTICS:

Statistics can be broken down into two broad areas, **descriptive statistics** and **inferential statistics**. The area of descriptive statistics deals with the collection and organization of data. This is followed by summarization in the form of averages and other such calculations involving use of the actual data collected. Inferential statistics deals with making predictions or drawing inferences based on the data collected and the values calculated under the descriptive area. In this chapter we will deal primarily with the area of descriptive statistics.

QUANTITATIVE VS QUALITATIVE DATA:

There are two types of **data** that may be collected. These two types are **quantitative** and **qualitative** data. Quantitative data involves quantities, amounts or measurements. This type of data is primarily numerical in nature. Qualitative data are generally non-numerical. Such information as color or shape are examples of qualitative data.

POPULATION DATA VS SAMPLE DATA:

Two other commonly used terms are **population** and **sample** data sets. If you are collecting and are able to get 100% of the information possible then you are dealing with a population. However, if you cannot get all possible information (this is usually the case), then you are dealing with a sample data set, i.e.

For example, suppose that you wish to do two surveys. One survey asks all of the students in your class for their height. If it is possible to get an answer from every student in your class, this is a population set. If you were to do the same survey for the entire college, you would not have any assurance that you could ask every single student. This would the be a sample data set. Most data sets are sample sets.

When population data sets are being used for calculations, etc., Greek letters will be used as abbreviations for quantities in formulas. If a sample data set is being considered, then common English letters will be used to stand for quantities in formulas. Another difference is that you can know all about a population but you cannot know all about a sample which is, by its very nature, known to be incomplete information. Thus, when calculations are done, care must be taken to be sure whether the data set is a sample or a population. Statements made about sample data sets are often inferential or inexact. Statements made about true population data sets can be exact since it is assumed that all possible information is available.

LEVELS OF DATA:

Data collected can ba categorized into one of four levels. In ascending order of complexity these are: **nominal level data, ordinal level data, interval level data and ratio level data.** Depending upon the level of the data that is being collected more or less calculation and estimation may be done. The following chart may be helpful in categorizing data.

LEVEL	DEFINITION	EXAMPLES
NOMINAL	name only, generally non-numerical, no meaningful order	colors, sex (M or F), social security number
ORDINAL	a meaningful ordering is possible, may still be non-numerical	answers such as high, medium, and low, on a scale of 1 to 10
INTERVAL	meaningful order and definite differences between values, no "real" zero value	shoe size, year born
RATIO	meaningful order, definite differences between values and "real" zeroes exist	age, height (or lengths in general), weights, volumes, concentrations

Practice Problem Set 7.1:

Suppose that you were asked to answer each of the following questions on a survey. Answer them appropriately and then answer the following questions for each question. a. Is the data **quantitative or qualitative**? b. What **level** data would the answers be?

1. What color are your eyes?

2. How tall are you?

3. In what year were you born?

4. How old are you?

5. How many sit ups can you do in 30 seconds?

6. Would you describe your anxiety level with respect to this chapter on statistics as high, medium or low?

7. How many kilograms does this book weigh?

8. Are you male or female?

9. What size shoe do you wear?

10. How many brothers and sisters do you have all together?

11. What is your numerical average for this course at this time?

12. What letter grade do you expect to earn for this course?

13. What is your telephone number?

7.2 BASIC DESCRIPTIVE STATISTICS

One of the most common statistical calculations done with data is finding **averages**. Averages are sometime called **measures of central tendency**. This means that an average is trying to describe numbers near the center of a list or group. If data is of interval or ratio level, then averages are simple to find. If, however, the data is of lower level, nominal or ordinal, then care must be exercised. Some data set may not have an average value if the level is low enough.

There are several values that can be calculated that are all called "averages." What follows are three of the most common.

THE MEAN AVERAGE

When most people hear the word "average" they think of adding a series of numbers and then dividing to find an average. This is what the **"mean average"** is.

$$\text{Mean Average} = \frac{\text{total of all the numbers}}{\text{the number of numbers}}$$

Since the mean average is so commonly used, it is given its own special symbol in statistics. This symbol is the letter "x" with a line over it like this, $\bar{x}$. This symbol is called **X-bar**. In statistics individual pieces of data are called "x." We can write the formula for calculating the mean average using all mathematical symbols as follows:

$$\bar{x} = \frac{\sum x}{n}$$

In the above formula, n = the number of numbers added, x represents the individual numbers and the Greek letter sigma, $\sum$, is a summation symbol and means "add 'em all up."

✎ **NOTE:** Not all levels of data have mean averages. For example, if the data is a set of colors (nominal level data), then a mean average cannot be found. This is because the colors cannot be added up. Similarly, ordinal level data will not have a mean average. Only interval and ratio level data have mean averages.

THE MEDIAN

Another common measure of central tendency is called the **median**. Like the median in a highway, the median of a set of data is the one in the middle after the data is placed in a meaningful order, such as highest to lowest. Since ordinal, interval and ratio levels of data may all be ordered, the median may be found for any of these levels of data. However, since nominal level data cannot be placed in any meaningful order, no median may be found for this level of data. Unlike the mean average, the median has no commonly agreed upon symbol or abbreviation.

THE MODE

If any of the data are repeated in the list, then the **mode** is the most often repeated piece of data. If several pieces of data are repeated and no one piece is repeated more than any other then, there are several modes possible. If no piece is repeated or all are repeated the same number of times then, there is no mode. Since repetition is the only requirement here, all levels of data may have a mode or modes.

There are other averages or measures of central tendency possible, such as weighted means. However, this is not a complete statistics course so we will limit our scope to these three.

Example 7.1: Find the mean, median and mode for the following set of data:

$$2, 4, 6, 9, 3, 4, 5, 8, 7, 4, 3$$

The mean average will be found by adding these numbers and then dividing the total by eleven, the number of numbers.

$$\bar{x} \;=\; \frac{\sum x}{n} \;=\; \frac{2+4+6+9+3+4+5+8+7+4+3}{11} \;=\; \frac{55}{11}$$

$$\bar{x} \;=\; 5$$

The median cannot be found until the numbers are sorted into some order, like lowest to highest:

$$2, 3, 3, 4, 4, 4, 5, 6, 7, 8, 9$$
$$\wedge$$

Now the number in the middle of the list is the median. This number is marked above.

$$\text{Median} = 4$$

The mode is the most often repeated number(s), if any, in   the list. It is true that both 3's and 4's are repeated but, there are more 4's, thus:

$$\text{Mode} = 4$$

✍ **NOTE:** An average is supposed to tell us what numbers near the center of the list of data are like or close to. In this case, all of the various averages agree fairly well. A number near the center of this list is close to a value of 4 or 5.

Example 7.2: Find the mean, median and mode for the following·set of data:

Five people in the class have blue eyes, seven have brown, two hazel and one green. (five blue, seven brown, two hazel, one green)

Even though there are numbers associated with this data, the actual data is colors of eyes and so, since we cannot add up colors, there is **no mean average**!

The colors can be placed in alphabetical order but that is   not a meaningful order since there is no inherent order to   eye color (i.e., no one color is better or should necessarily come first or last). Thus, there is **no median**!

NOTES

Some of the colors are repeated. There are more people with brown eyes than any other color, thus:

Mode = brown eyes

Example 7.3: Find the mean, median and mode for the following set of data:

$$20, 30, 30, 40, 50, 70$$
$$\wedge$$

$$\bar{x} = \frac{20 + 30 + 30 + 40 + 50 + 70}{6} = \frac{240}{6}$$

$$\bar{x} = 40$$

The median's location is marked on the list of numbers (they are already sorted this time.) Any time a list of numbers contains an even number of numbers, the location of the median will be between two numbers. To find the median in this situation, add the two numbers that are on each side of the median and divide by two:

Median = 35

Mode = 30

THE "BEST" AVERAGE

If you are requested to report one average value, the mean average is generally considered to be the "best" average. This is because every number in the data set is used in calculating its value. The value of the median is determined by two numbers at most, in the list. The mode may even be near one end of the list and, since an average is supposed to indicate what values near the center of the list are like, may not be a good measure of central tendency at all. In fact, there may be no mode for some data sets.

One case in which the mean may not be the "best" average is when the data set contains a few numbers that are either extremely large or small compared to the bulk of the other data. In this case, the median is usually reported.

Example 7.4: Find the "best" average for the following data set:

$$2, 2, 3, 4, 5, 7, 8, 9, 12, 13, 45.$$
$$\wedge$$

First, let's calculate all three averages:

the mean average: $\bar{x} = 110/11 = 10$

the median: median = 7

the mode: mode = 2

In this case, the one high value, 45, has pulled the mean   average off-center toward the higher end of the list. Thus, the median, 7, is closer to the value of numbers near the middle of the list than is the mean of 10. Note that the mode of 2 is nowhere near the middle values of this list.

NOTES

NOTES

Practice Problem Set 7.2:

1. Find the mean, median and mode for each of the following sets of data:

(a) 2, 3, 5, 5, 6, 7, 8, 9, 11, 15

(b) 200, 305, 411, 516, 576, 599, 602

(c) 2.3, 4.5, 5.6, 5.6, 7.9, 8.2, 9.0, 15.6

2. If you were to do a survey of your friends in order to determine their favorite TV show, what average could you calculate or report for your results?

3. The number of laboratory workers in North Carolina industries has increased from 3000 to 4880 over a period of five years. Calculate the average annual rate of increase.

4. What is the "best" average for the following data and why?

2, 3, 300, 308, 400, 450, 450, 490, 500, 580, 604

5. During a long period of rain, the meteorology class at a   local college recorded the amount of rainfall per hour with the results listed below. What was the average hourly rate of rainfall over the 24 hour period covered by the data?

5 ml, 3 ml, 6 ml, 6 ml, 10 ml, 4 ml, 1 ml, 0 ml, 0 ml, 0 ml, 1 ml, 0 ml, 3 ml, 4 ml, 4 ml, 7 ml, 8 ml, 12 ml, 10 ml, 1 ml, 5 ml, 0 ml, 0 ml, 1 ml.

7.3 VARIATION (DISPERSION)

NOTES

Take a look at the following sets of data. Note that the three sets are <u>not</u> identical and yet their mean average and median values are the same. The same can be true for large data sets with many different values.

DATA SET #	ONE	TWO	THREE
	5	6	7
	5	5	6
	5	5	5
	5	5	4
	5	4	3
Sum	25	25	25
Mean Average	5	5	5
Median	5	5	5

To report only the averages for these data sets may lead someone to conclude that the underlying data are identical. This would be an incorrect conclusion. This means that we need another measure that tells us about <u>differences between and among</u> the data.

When values of various numbers are not identical, we say that the numbers **vary**. There are two commonly used **measures of variation (or dispersion)** between numbers in a set of data. These two measures are the **range** of the data and the **standard deviation** of the data.

NOTES

RANGE

The range of a set of data is easily calculated as follows:

Range (R) = highest value - lowest value.

The range of the three data set above are as follows:

Set One: R = 5 - 5 = 0
Set Two: R = 6 - 4 = 2
Set Three: R = 7 - 3 = 4

Once the range is known for each set, it is then clear that the three data sets are <u>not identical</u> since the values of the range are different in each case.

As a measure of variation the range, like the median, has limited use. It is calculated using only two of the numbers from the list. A better measure of variation would be one that used all the numbers in the list to aid in its determination. The standard deviation is such a measure.

STANDARD DEVIATION

The **standard deviation**, denoted by the letter **s**, of a set of numbers is a little more complicated to calculate than the range. Setting up the data in table form, sorted highest to lowest will make calculation easier. The formula for calculating a sample standard deviation value is:

$$s = \sqrt{\frac{\Sigma(x-\bar{x})^2}{n-1}}$$

✎   **NOTE:** This is the formula for a sample standard deviation. Since most laboratory procedures involve samples, as opposed to population, this is the most often used formula.

The procedure is as follows:

Step 1: Calculate the mean average, $\bar{x}$

Step 2: Subtract the value of the mean from each number, x, in the list, $(x - \bar{x})$.

Step 3: Square the resulting values to eliminate all negative signs, $(x - \bar{x})^2$. (This is mathematical "slight of hand" to avoid a sum of zero.)

Step 4: Add up all of the squared values, $\Sigma(x - \bar{x})^2$.

Step 5: Divide the result of Step 4 by the number of numbers in the original data set minus one $(n - 1)$.

Step 6: Find the square root of the number found in Step 5. This result is the standard deviation, s.

This seems like a long process, but it really goes very quickly if you practice a little. Setting up a chart, as in Example 7.5 below, makes the calculation easier. In lab situations where such calculations are done routinely, you will probably use a computer program to do this for you automatically.

Example 7.5: Let's find the standard deviation for Set Three on the previous chart.

x	$\bar{x}$	$(x - \bar{x})$	$(x - \bar{x})^2$
7	5	2	4
6	5	1	1
5	5	0	0
4	5	-1	1
3	5	-2	4
	Sums, Σ	0	10

The <u>standard deviation</u> is the square root of 10 divided by 5-1,

$$s = \sqrt{(10/4)} = 1.58$$

COEFFICIENT OF VARIATION

The **coefficient of variation (CV)** of a sample set is calculated by dividing the standard deviation by the mean average and multiplying the result by 100% as follows:

$$CV = \frac{\text{standard deviation}}{\text{mean average}} \times 100\% = \frac{s}{\bar{x}} \times 100\%$$

NOTES

NOTES

The use of a coefficient of variation value is growing in many laboratory areas. For example the CDC (Center for Disease Control) has set a CV of 3% as the nationwide standard for measurements of cholesterol values by all clinical and testing laboratories. The CDC sent a controlled sample of cholesterol to all testing laboratories and told them that they had to be within 3% (i.e., ±3%) of the target value for the sample as determined by the CDC. Labs that did not come within this value had to calibrate their instruments so that they did fall within the required CV range.

Another use of the CV value is when trying to duplicate a manufacturer's result in your lab. For example, if you make two samples and they are not exactly the same as the manufacturer's specification, how do you know when you are too far off for the result to be usable? One way is to find the percent difference between your lowest and highest value. The percent difference is found as follows:

$$\text{percent difference} = ([\text{low - high}] / \text{high}) \times 100\%$$

If the percent of difference is less than or equal to the CV, that is within ±CV, then your samples are 'ok.'

Many manufacturers of laboratory testing devices routinely include a value for CV as part of the specifications for their devices. For example, the Unopette Microcollection System[1] is a diagnostic reagent system for the enumeration of erythrocytes in whole blood samples. In the circular that accompanies this device, expected levels of performance are given. Based on 40 determinations or counts, the device should yield a mean of 5.67×10^6 erythrocytes/mm^3, with a standard deviation of $\pm 0.20 \times 10^6$ and a coefficient of variation of 3.5%. These values allow a lab to check the precision of the method being used.

[1]The Unopette Microcollection System is manufactured by Becton-Dickinson and Company of Rutherford, New Jersy.

Practice Problem Set 7.3:

1. Calculate the range (R) and standard deviation (s) of the following set of numbers:

1419, 1410, 1410, 1403, 1396, 1389, 1400, 1380, 1422.

2. Calculate the range and standard deviation of the following:

15.2 16.7 15.8 14.6 18.1 17.2 18.0
14.8 17.6 18.2 16.9 17.3 16.5 18.2

3. What does it mean if the standard deviation of a set of numbers is zero? (Hint: see Data Set Three in the first chart in this section.

4. What does it mean if the range is zero?

5. Assume that a series of glucose concentration measurements have been done. The mean average for this series was determined to be 64 mg/dl with a standard deviation of 2.7 mg/dl. What is the CV for this set of data?

NOTES

7.4 NORMAL DISTRIBUTIONS

Often, sets of data may be very large. This may be due to large samples or to the accumulation of data over some time. In either case, organizing the data into tables or graphs is commonly done. This more compact presentation of the data makes interpretation of trends, etc., easier. Of course, statisticians have their own names for things. A common way of sorting data is to construct a **frequency distribution**. Frequency distributions are tables that result from sorting large groups of numbers into a limited number of categories or groupings.

For example, in a set of numbers that are all less than 100, they might be sorted by 10's. This means that all the numbers would end up in one of ten categories. The **frequency** of each category would be the count of the numbers that ended up in each group (i.e., how many in 1-10, how many in 11-20, etc.)

A frequency distribution can then become the basis for a graph. For example, each category could be represented by one bar of a bar graph. The height of the bar would correspond to the frequency for that category. Looking at the graph tells you how the original numbers are distributed and whether there is a clustering of numbers in certain categories.

Many sets of data fit one particular curve when graphed. This curve is called a **normal curve or bell curve** (see Figure #1.) Notice that most of the data in this curve clusters around the mean, while few values are a lot larger or smaller than the mean average.

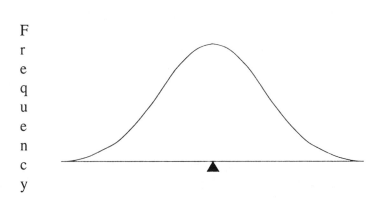

F
r
e
q
u
e
n
c
y

Figure #1

Many types of data should fit this general shape when graphed. As an example, let's suppose that you asked as many students as possible at your college how old they were. This would be a large data set. If the ages were sorted in some way, such as all those age 16-20, 21-25, 26-30, etc., and then graphed, what would you expect the shape of the graph to be? There would be a few students much younger than the mean average age of a student at the college, and a few much older. However, most would be close to the same age. That is, the ages would cluster around the average age. The graph should be approximately bell shaped or normally distributed.

If sample data are carefully gathered and the values produce a normal curve, then the probability is high that the population from which the sample was taken is also normally distributed. The normal curve can then be used as a **predictor** of characteristics of the population in regard to the data collected.

In laboratory and industry areas, normal distributions and other statistical analysis of processes and products, are commonly used as part of **quality control** operations. There are several names used to indicate this. For example, you may have heard of **statistical process control (SPC)**, or **statistical quality control (SQC)**, or **total quality management (TQM)**, or any number of similar names. Many laboratory workers are part of the quality assurance departments of industries all over the world. Some familiarity with normal curves and their common characteristics will be very useful to most lab technicians.

NOTES

NOTES

NORMAL CURVES AND PROBABILITY

If a population is truly normally distributed, then estimations and predictions can be made based on comparisons with a standard normal curve. On a standard normal curve, the **probability** that a certain value will occur can be assigned a **percentage chance** based on its value as compared to the mean average and the standard deviation of the set of data.

A base line is set up using the value of the mean average as the central number and then adding the value of the standard deviation to the right and subtracting it to the left as follows:

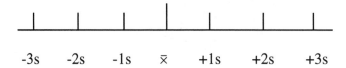

$\qquad$ -3s $\qquad$ -2s $\qquad$ -1s $\qquad$ $\bar{x}$ $\qquad$ +1s $\qquad$ +2s $\qquad$ +3s

It is assumed that the normal curve encompasses all possible values for a given set of data, that is 100%. If the data are truly normally distributed, then we would expect to find approximately 68.3% of all values in the range from -1s to +1s (see Figure #2 below). If we extend the range from -2s to +2s, then 95.5% of the data should be included. By the time we are out to the -3s to +3s range, then about 99.7% of the data should be included.

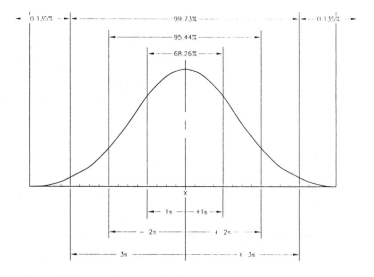

Normal Curve Probabilities
Figure #2

In the laboratory setting, normal curves are often very useful. However, they are <u>not</u> the only possible shape that the data may have on a graph. Many other shapes or distributions are possible but are beyond the scope of this text. If this area interests you, perhaps you should consider taking a true statistics course.

NOTES

7.5 CONTROL CHARTS

In modern chemical laboratories and related industries, control charts, based on the properties of the normal curve, are commonly used. These charts go by many names including **Shewhart charts** (named after the person who was the main developer of this type of chart), or **x-bar charts** (named after the mean average), or **Levey-Jennings charts**, or any of several other names. All of these charts are essentially the same. Figure #3 shows a sample of such a chart.

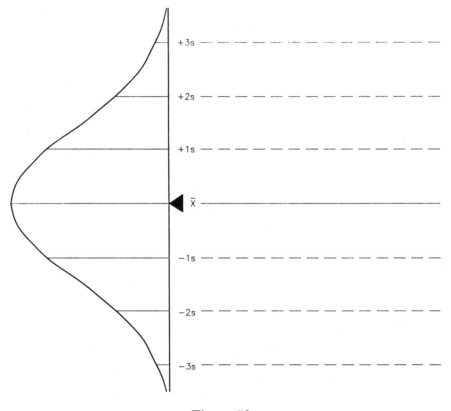

Figure #3

The Levey-Jennings chart above is based on a normal curve turned on its side. The center line of the chart represents the value of the mean average for the data. Each of the lines above the center line represent the value of the mean plus one, two and three standard deviations values respectively. Those below represent the values of the mean minus one, two and three standard deviations respectively. This is the same as the base line for the normal curve, $\bar{x}$, ±1s, ±2s, and ±3s (see Figure #2 in the previous section).

A control chart can be established for any ongoing process in a laboratory. Once established, results of testing the process today or for the current product run can easily be compared to the previous day(s) production. This is done taking samples of a product run and comparing its characteristics to the established criteria for the product based on long experience or established product norms. This is often the function of the quality assurance department at a lab or chemical industry. Run-by-run or hour-by-hour or other regular sample testing may be done and the results plotted onto the control chart forming an ongoing record of the quality of the product being manufactured (see Figure #4 for such a chart).

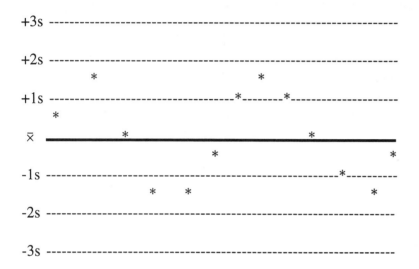

Control Chart
Figure #4

Notice how the series of marks, *, representing data recorded, meander back and forth across the center line. This is a chart that shows the normal variation that one would expect to see in a well run process. Control charts let us track processes of many kinds over time. The time between successive data points on the chart may vary according to the process. They may be every hour, every shift or product run, or any other convenient time.

If a control chart is based on good data then it may be used to indicate changes in the product or process being tracked. In other words, if things begin to go "wrong," they will show up on the chart in some way. As each point is plotted, it is also necessary to note the time of the plot, the sample used (for example a product run number, batch number, etc.) and the machine or lab station from which the sample was derived. This will allow tracking of any problems discovered.

NOTES

NOTES

INTERPRETATION OF CONTROL CHARTS

How do you tell from the chart that a process has started to go wrong? One of the simplest standards used is to set **control limits** on the chart. These are usually set at +2s for the **upper control limit** and at -2s for the **lower control limit**. The dotted lines at these points represent the 95.5% confidence interval mentioned in the section of this chapter on the normal curve. If a point is plotted outside of these limits, the chances are slim (only 2.25% above +2s and 2.25% below -2s) that the data meet the product specifications. Something is **out of control** in the process and a second look needs to be made to correct the apparent problem.

There are other ways to identify problems with a process using the control chart. What follows are three charts (Figures #5, #6 and #7) showing other identifiable problems on control charts. REMEMBER: a "good" chart should meander back an forth across the center line and no points should be above +2s or below -2s.

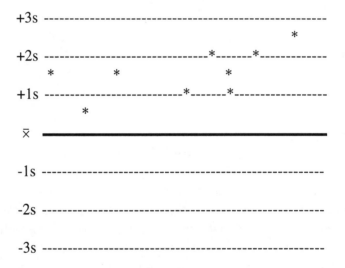

Figure #5 A Shift

A **shift** in the center of the process is shown in the figure above. Note that the data points are meandering back an forth around the +2s line and not the mean. This shows that the average value for the data being plotted has shifted to a higher value than the original x-bar value. A shift usually occurs very abruptly in most process and becomes obvious after several sets of data have been plotted. The QC technician making the control chart may then check back to see what was changed to cause the shift.

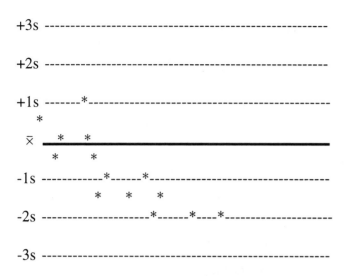

Figure #6 A Trend

Notice here that the points are headed steadily in one direction. They do not meander around any of the lines. This **trend** downward indicates a steady drift in the process being tracked. If the trend continues, all of the product being sampled will soon be outside the control limits. Something in this process is out of adjustment and needs to be fixed.

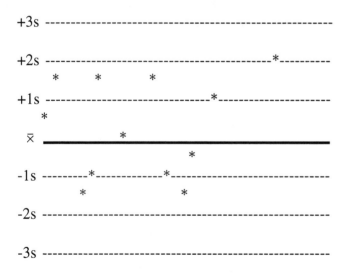

Figure #7 Imprecision

The points on this chart jump wildly from one plotting to the next. This is not normal because there is too much variability shown between successive measurements. This **imprecision** could be the result of poor technique of a lab technician (as in improper pipetting, etc.) or of lack of attention to details.

NOTES

The four <u>trouble indicators</u> shown above: (1) points outside of control limits, (2) a shift in the value of the mean average, (3) a trend of the data either steadily upwards or downwards and (4) imprecision shown by wild fluctuations between successive data points, are commonly used by many industries around the world. However, these four indicators are not precise enough in many clinical or industrial areas. More precise sets of <u>rules for chart evaluation</u> have been developed.

MULTIRULE SYSTEMS FOR CONTROL CHART INTERPRE-TATION

Since control charts can indicate a number of different problems, several rules are needed. Hence the name **multirule system**. One set of such rules commonly used in QC laboratories is **Westgard's multirule system**.[2] Use of these rules will generally lead to less chance of falsely rejecting acceptable product runs or lab test results than the four indicators previously listed. When used in conjunction with Levey-Jennings charts the same confidence interval is used, +2s to -2s, the 95.5% confidence interval.

The following chart lists the Westgard rules. There may be some slight variation in these rules as applied in various labs but, most are almost exactly the same as those listed.

[2]Westgard, J. O., Barry, P. L., Hunt, M. R., Groth, T. *A multi-rule shewhart chart for quality control in clinical chemistry*; <u>Clinical Chemistry</u>; vol. 27., p. 493-501; 1981.

WESTGARD MULTI-RULES

Rule 1-2S: One value on the control chart exceeds the mean by more than 2 standard deviations but less than 3s. This value can exceed the mean in either the upward or downward direction. {Note: this is the "red flag" rule.}

Rule 1-3S: One value on the control chart exceeds the mean by more than 3 standard deviations in either the upward or downward direction.

Rule 2-2S: Two consecutive values on the control chart exceed the mean by more than 2 standard deviations but less than 3s. These two values must be consecutive and lie on the same side of the mean.

Rule R-4S: The difference between two consecutive values on the control chart is greater than four standard deviations. These two points have assay values in opposite directions from each other, and the difference between the two spans at least four standard deviations.

Rule 10x: Ten consecutive values on the control chart are on the same side of the mean (whether or not any of them exceed two standard deviations.)

In the original Westgard multirule system, Rule 1-2S is a red flag that indicates a possible change in relative accuracy or precision. If Rule 1-2S is violated, this does not always indicate an error in measurement. The remaining rules are first applied to the data. If there is no violation of any of the other rules, the value causing the violation of Rule 1-2S is then considered acceptable and assay results are released.

<u>Points to remember</u>: (1) A violation of Rule 1-3S is always a reason for rejection. This is due to the fact that 99.7% of all values should fall <u>within</u> three standard deviations of the mean average. A value outside of that range is improbable and thus probably results from an abnormal measurement of some form. (2) Values must <u>exceed</u> the limits to be considered a violation. A value that is plotted on a limit line is not a violation of the limit. (3) Rules R-4S and 4-1S cannot be applied unless the red flag Rule 1-2S has been observed first.

NOTES

NOTES

The flow chart on the next page may help you to work your way through the Westgard multirule system. The flow chart also indicates the probable type of error, systematic or random, that is the likely cause of the rule violation.

Different industries use sets of multirules similar to the Westgard rules. The variations can be significant depending upon the type of industry and the property being tracked by the control chart.

FLOW CHART FOR THE WESTGARD MULTIRULE SYSTEM:

Is one value outside 2S? (Rule 1-2S) YES ⇨ Check other rules for possible violation

NO
⇩
Accept Run.

⇩

Is one value outside of 3S? (Rule 1-3S) YES ⇨ Reject Run Random Error

NO
⇩
Are 2 values outside of 2S? (Rule 2-2S) YES ⇨ Reject Run Systematic Error

NO
⇩
Is the difference between any 2 values > 4S? (Rule R-4S) YES ⇨ Reject Run Random Error

NO
⇩
Are 4 consecutive values outside +1S or -1S? YES ⇨ Reject Run Systematic Error

NO
⇩
Are there 10 consecutive values on one side of the mean? (Rule 10x) YES ⇨ Reject Run Systematic Error

NO
⇩
Accept Run

NOTES

NOTES

✎ **NOTE:** In all cases you should check <u>all</u> of the rules for violation. With a little practice this will become very easy to do.

Practice Problem Set 7.5:

1. Construct a Levy-Jennings chart using the following data collected in a laboratory. Then determine if any Westgard rules have been violated.

   Mean average = 7.6 mmol/L
   Standard Deviation = 0.1 mmol/L

   Data to be plotted in order collected: 7.4, 7.5, 7.7, 7.4, 7.3, 7.6, 7.5, 7.8, 7.9, 7.9.

2. What follows here is a series of simple control charts. The dark central line represents the location of the mean average for the data, and the upper and lower dotted lines represent +2s and -2s respectively. The points representing the data collected have been connected by lines to make them show up better on the small scale drawings. Decide if any of the Westgard multirules have been violated and, if so, which one(s).

2A)

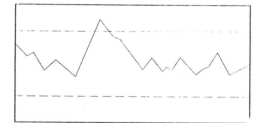

2B)

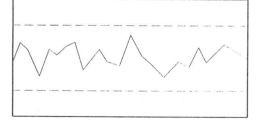

2C)

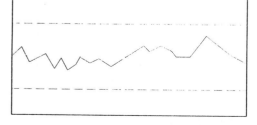

NOTES

2D)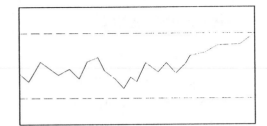

3. Assume that a you are working in a facility that is producing solutions for use by other labs. One of these solutions is to have a concentration of 7.00 mg/dl of ammonium nitrate. As part of the QC team you periodically test batches of this solution and find that the concentration of ammonium nitrate is normally distributed with a mean average of 7.00 mg/dl as required, and a standard deviation of 0.25 mg/dl. Using the normal curve drawn below, with the usual percentages as previously described, answer each of the following questions:

A) What is the percentage chance that the next sample tested will have a concentration of less than 7.00 mg/dl?

B) What is the percent chance that a sample will have a concentration that is between 7.50 and 6.75 mg/dl?

C) What about a concentration that is less than 6.50 mg/dl?

D) What about a concentration greater than 7.50 mg/dl?

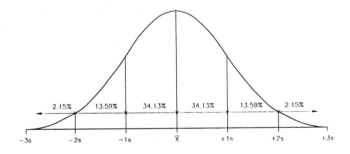

CHAPTER 7: SUMMARY

KEY TERMS TO REMEMBER:

statistics | descriptive
inferential | quantitative
qualitative | data
population | sample
average | mean
median | mode
standard deviation | bell curve
frequency | nominal
normal distribution | interval
ordinal | control limits
ratio
levels of data
coefficient of variation
measure of central tendency
Levey-Jennings chart
Westgard rules

FORMULAS TO REMEMBER

Mean Average:
$$\overline{X} = \frac{\Sigma X}{n}$$

Standard Deviation:
$$s = \sqrt{\frac{\Sigma (x-\overline{x})^2}{n-1}}$$

Coefficient of Variation:
$$CV = \frac{s}{\overline{x}} \; X \; 100\%$$

NOTES

CHAPTER REVIEW PROBLEMS

1. Differentiate between a population and a sample.

2. Differentiate between quantitative and qualitative data.

3. Why is it important to know the level of the data that you are collecting?

4. Differentiate between descriptive and inferential statistics. When you did problem number three in practice problem set 7.5, which area of statistics were you working in?

For each of the following tell if the data is (A) quantitative or qualitative data and (B) the level of data (nominal, ordinal, interval or ratio.)

5. The manufacturer of the car you drive.

6. The capacity of a flask measured in ml.

7. A substance concentration in mg/dl.

8. The temperature of a sample in the lab.

For each of the following find the mean, median and mode. Of the three averages, determine which would be the "best" in each case and why.

9. 7.0 ml, 7.2 ml, 6.8 ml, 7.2 ml, 7.1 ml, 6.9 ml, 7.3 ml.

10. 2, 3, 5, 6, 8, 2, 4, 6, 7, 1, 0, 2, 0, 3, 50.

11. red, blue, green, red, yellow, blue, blue, white.

SUGGESTED LABORATORY EXERCISES

LABORATORY EXERCISE 1: ANALYZING DATA

Your instructor may supply you with some laboratory data collected at a local chemical industry, clinical testing lab or other such facility. The instructor might even wish to have you collect a series of data for analysis.

The data should be analyzed in as much statistical detail as possible including averages, variation, and a Levey-Jennings chart.

NOTES

NOTES

APPENDIXES

I.   **Commonly Used Calculator Keys**

II. **Metric Units**

III. **Periodic Table of Elements**

IV. **Table of Atomic Masses (Weights) Based On Carbon-12**

V.   **Names and Valences of Common Ions**

VI. **Optical Density/Transmission Table**

VII. **Answers to Practice Problems**

I. COMMONLY USED CALCULATOR KEYS

KEY	FUNCTION*
SHIFT or 2nd	Allows access to calculator functions printed above the keys
+/-	Used to change the sign of a number or enter a negative number into the calculator
$\sqrt{}$	Used to take the square root of a number
x^2	Used to raise a number to the second power (square a number) Enter 10^2 as: 10 x^2
y^x or x^y	Used to raise a number to an exponential power. Enter 5^3 as: 5 y^x 3 =
EXP or EE	Used to enter a number written in scientific notation into the calculator. Enter 3×10^2 as: 3 EE 2
log	Used to find the logarithm of a number base 10
ln	Used to find the natural logarithm of a number (base e)
a^b/c	Used to enter a fraction into the calculator. Enter ½ as: 1 a^b/c 2
$\bar{x}$	Gives the arithmetic mean of a set of data when the calculator is in the statistics mode
δ or δ_n	Gives population standard deviation for a set of data when the calculator is in the statistics mode
δ_{n-1} or s	Gives the sample standard deviation for a set of data when the calculator is in the statistics mode

* The keystrokes and keys on individual calculators vary according to brands. The list above is a general resource to help you quickly find an explanation of certain keys. For complete information, consult the manual that accompanied your particular calculator.

II. METRIC UNITS

PREFIXES AND VALUES FOR SI UNITS

PREFIX	SYMBOL	NUMERICAL VALUE		
giga	G	10^9	=	1,000,000,000
mega	M	10^6	=	1,000,000
kilo	k	10^3	=	1,000
hecto	h	10^2	=	100
deka	da	10^1	=	10
(metric unit)	-	10^0	=	1
deci	d	10^{-1}	=	0.1
centi	c	10^{-2}	=	0.01
milli	m	10^{-3}	=	0.001
micro	μ	10^{-6}	=	0.000001
nano	n	10^{-9}	=	0.000000001
pico	p	10^{-12}	=	0.000000000001

COMMON LABORATORY MEASUREMENT UNITS AND ABBREVIATIONS

MASS	LENGTH	VOLUME
kilogram (kg)	meter (m)	liter (l)
gram (g)	centimeter (cm)	deciliter (dl)
centigram (cg)	millimeter (mm)	milliliter (ml)
milligram (mg)	micrometer (μm)	microliter (μl)
microgram (μg)	or	nanoliter (nl)
nanogram (ng)	micron (μ)	
picogram (pg)	nanometer (nm)	

III. PERIODIC TABLE OF ELEMENTS

1A																	Noble gases 8A
1 H 1.008	Alkaline earth metals ↓ 2A		Transition metals									3A	4A	5A	6A	Halogens ↓ 7A	2 He 4.003
3 Li 6.941	4 Be 9.012											5 B 10.81	6 C 12.01	7 N 14.01	8 O 16.00	9 F 19.00	10 Ne 20.18
11 Na 22.99	12 Mg 24.31											13 Al 26.98	14 Si 28.09	15 P 30.97	16 S 32.06	17 Cl 35.45	18 Ar 39.95
19 K 39.10	20 Ca 40.08	21 Sc 44.96	22 Ti 47.88	23 V 50.94	24 Cr 52.00	25 Mn 54.94	26 Fe 55.85	27 Co 58.93	28 Ni 58.69	29 Cu 63.55	30 Zn 65.38	31 Ga 69.72	32 Ge 72.59	33 As 74.92	34 Se 78.96	35 Br 79.90	36 Kr 83.80
37 Rb 85.47	38 Sr 87.62	39 Y 88.91	40 Zr 91.22	41 Nb 92.91	42 Mo 95.94	43 Tc (98)	44 Ru 101.1	45 Rh 102.9	46 Pd 106.4	47 Ag 107.9	48 Cd 112.4	49 In 114.8	50 Sn 118.7	51 Sb 121.8	52 Te 127.6	53 I 126.9	54 Xe 131.9
55 Cs 132.9	56 Ba 137.3	57 La* 138.9	72 Hf 178.5	73 Ta 180.9	74 W 183.9	75 Re 186.2	76 Os 190.2	77 Ir 192.2	78 Pt 195.1	79 Au 197.0	80 Hg 200.6	81 Tl 204.4	82 Pb 207.2	83 Bi 209.0	84 Po (209)	85 At (210)	86 Rn (222)
87 Fr (223)	88 Ra 226	89 Ac† (227)	104 Unq	105 Unp	106 Unh	107 Uns	108 Uno	109 Une					metals ← → nonmetals				

*Lanthanides	58 Ce 140.1	59 Pr 140.9	60 Nd 144.2	61 Pm (145)	62 Sm 150.4	63 Eu 152.0	64 Gd 157.3	65 Tb 158.9	66 Dy 162.5	67 Ho 164.9	68 Er 167.3	69 Tm 168.9	70 Yb 173.0	71 Lu 175.0
†Actinides	90 Th 232.0	91 Pa (231)	92 U 238.0	93 Np (237)	94 Pu (244)	95 Am (243)	96 Cm (247)	97 Bk (247)	98 Cf (251)	99 Es (252)	100 Fm (257)	101 Md (258)	102 No (259)	103 Lr (260)

Alkali metals

IV. TABLE OF ATOMIC MASSES (WEIGHTS) BASED ON CARBON-12

Name	Symbol	Atomic Number	Atomic Mass	Name	Symbol	Atomic Number	Atomic Mass
Actinium	Ac	89	(227)*	Molybdenum	Mo	42	95.94
Aluminum	Al	13	26.98154	Neodymium	Nd	60	144.24
Americium	Am	95	(243)*	Neon	Ne	10	20.179
Antimony	Sb	51	121.75	Neptunium	Np	93	237.0482**
Argon	Ar	18	39.948	Nickel	Ni	28	58.71
Arsenic	As	33	74.9216	Niobium	Nb	41	92.9064
Astatine	At	85	(210)*	Nitrogen	N	7	14.0067
Barium	Ba	56	137.54	Nobelium	No	102	(259)*
Berkelium	Bk	97	(247)*	Osmium	Os	76	190.2
Beryllium	Be	4	9.01218	Oxygen	O	8	15.9994
Bismuth	Bi	83	208.9804	Palladium	Pd	46	106.4
Boron	B	5	10.81	Phosphorus	P	15	30.97376
Bromine	Br	35	79.904	Platinum	Pt	78	195.09
Cadmium	Cd	48	112.40	Plutonium	Pu	94	(244)*
Calcium	Ca	20	40.08	Polonium	Po	84	(210)*
Californium	Cf	98	(251)*	Potassium	K	19	39.098
Carbon	C	6	12.011	Praseodymium	Pr	59	140.9077
Cerium	Ce	58	140.12	Promethium	Pm	61	(145)*
Cesium	Cs	55	132.9054	Protactinium	Pa	91	231.0359**
Chlorine	Cl	17	35.453	Radium	Ra	88	226.0254**
Chromium	Cr	24	51.996	Radon	Rn	86	(222)*
Cobalt	Co	27	58.9332	Rhenium	Re	75	186.2
Copper	Cu	29	63.546	Rhodium	Rh	45	102.9055
Curium	Cm	96	(247)*	Rubidium	Rb	37	85.4678
Dysprosium	Dy	66	162.50	Ruthenium	Ru	44	101.07
Einsteinium	Es	99	(252)*	Samarium	Sm	62	150.4
Erbium	Er	68	167.26	Scandium	Sc	21	44.9559
Europium	Eu	63	151.96	Selenium	Se	34	78.96
Fermium	Fm	100	(257)*	Silicon	Si	14	28.086
Fluorine	F	9	18.99840	Silver	Ag	47	107.868
Francium	Fr	87	(223)*	Sodium	Na	11	22.98977
Gadolinium	Gd	64	157.25	Strontium	Sr	38	87.62
Gallium	Ga	31	69.72	Sulfur	S	16	32.06
Germanium	Ge	32	72.59	Tantalum	Ta	73	180.9479
Gold	Au	79	196.9665	Technetium	Tc	43	98.9062**
Hafnium	Hf	72	178.49	Tellurium	Te	52	127.60
Helium	He	2	4.00260	Terbium	Tb	65	158.9254
Holmium	Ho	67	164.9304	Thallium	Tl	81	204.37
Hydrogen	H	1	1.0079	Thorium	Th	90	232.0381**
Indium	In	49	114.82	Thulium	Tm	69	168.9342
Iodine	I	53	126.9045	Tin	Sn	50	118.69
Iridium	Ir	77	192.22	Titanium	Ti	22	47.90
Iron	Fe	26	55.847	Tungsten	W	74	183.85
Krypton	Kr	36	83.80	Unnilhexium	Unh	106	(263)*
Lanthanum	La	57	138.9055	Unnilpentium	Unp	105	(262)*
Lawrencium	Lr	103	(260)*	Unnilquadium	Unq	104	(261)*
Lead	Pb	82	207.2	Uranium	U	92	238.029
Lithium	Li	3	6.941	Vanadium	V	23	50.9414
Lutetium	Lu	71	174.97	Xenon	Xe	54	131.30
Magnesium	Mg	12	24.305	Ytterbium	Yb	70	173.04
Manganese	Mn	25	54.9380	Yttrium	Y	39	88.9059
Mendelevium	Md	101	(258)*	Zinc	Zn	30	65.38
Mercury	Hg	80	200.59	Zirconium	Zr	40	91.22

* Mass number of most stable or best-known isotope
** Mass number of the isotope of longest half-life

V. NAMES AND VALENCES OF COMMON IONS

POSITIVE IONS

Valence +1

Ammonium	NH_4
Copper(I)	Cu
Hydrogen	H
Potassium	K
Silver	Ag
Sodium	Na

Valence +2

Barium	Ba
Cadmium	Cd
Calcium	Ca
Cobalt(II)	Co
Copper(II)	Cu
Iron(II)	Fe
Lead(II)	Pb
Magnesium	Mg
Manganese(II)	Mn
Mercury(II)	Hg
Nickel(II)	Ni
Tin(II)	Sn
Zinc	Zn

Valence +3

Aluminum	Al
Antimony(III)	Sb
Arsenic(III)	As
Bismuth(III)	Bi
Chromium(III)	Cr
Iron(III)	Fe
Titanium(III)	Ti

Valence +4

Manganese	Mn
Tin(IV)	Sn
Titanium(IV)	Ti

Valence +5

Antimony(V)	Sb
Arsenic(V)	As

NEGATIVE IONS

Valence -1

Acetate	$C_2H_3O_2$
Bromate	BrO_3
Bromide	Br
Chlorate	ClO_3
Chloride	Cl
Chlorite	ClO_2
Cyanide	CN
Fluoride	F
Hydride	H
Bicarbonate	HCO_3
Bisulfate	HSO_4
Bisulfite	HSO_3
Hydroxide	OH
Hypochlorite	ClO
Iodate	IO_3
Iodide	I
Nitrate	NO_3
Nitrite	NO_2
Perchlorate	ClO_4
Permanganate	MnO_4
Thiocyanate	SCN

Valence -2

Carbonate	CO_3
Chromate	CrO_4
Dichromate	Cr_2O_7
Oxalate	C_2O_4
Oxide	O
Peroxide	O_2
Silicate	SiO_3
Sulfate	SO_4
Sulfide	S
Sulfite	SO_3

Valence -3

Arsenate	AsO_4
Borate	BO_3
Phosphate	PO_4
Phosphite	PO_3

VI. OPTICAL DENSITY/TRANSMISSION TABLE

Formula: OD = -log T
where OD = optical density or absorbance
and T = % transmittance as a decimal

%T	OD(A)	%T	OD(A)	%T	OD(A)	%T	OD(A)
1.0	2.000	26.0	0.585	51.0	0.292	76.0	0.119
1.5	1.824	26.5	0.577	51.5	0.288	76.5	0.116
2.0	1.699	27.0	0.569	52.0	0.284	77.0	0.114
2.5	1.602	27.5	0.561	52.5	0.280	77.5	0.111
3.0	1.523	28.0	0.533	53.0	0.276	78.0	0.108
3.5	1.456	28.5	0.545	53.5	0.272	78.5	0.105
4.0	1.398	29.0	0.538	54.0	0.268	79.0	0.102
4.5	1.347	29.5	0.530	54.5	0.264	79.5	0.100
5.0	1.301	30.0	0.523	55.0	0.260	80.0	0.097
5.5	1.260	30.5	0.516	55.5	0.256	80.5	0.094
6.0	1.222	31.0	0.509	56.0	0.252	81.0	0.092
6.5	1.187	31.5	0.502	56.5	0.248	81.5	0.089
7.0	1.155	32.0	0.495	57.0	0.244	82.0	0.086
7.5	1.126	32.5	0.488	57.5	0.240	82.5	0.084
8.0	1.097	33.0	0.482	58.0	0.237	83.0	0.081
8.5	1.071	33.5	0.475	58.5	0.233	83.5	0.078
9.0	1.046	34.0	0.469	59.0	0.229	84.0	0.076
9.5	1.022	34.5	0.462	59.5	0.226	84.5	0.073
10.0	1.000	35.0	0.456	60.0	0.222	85.0	0.071
10.5	0.979	35.5	0.450	60.5	0.218	85.5	0.068
11.0	0.959	36.0	0.444	61.0	0.215	86.0	0.066
11.5	0.939	36.5	0.438	61.5	0.211	86.5	0.063
12.0	0.921	37.0	0.432	62.0	0.208	87.0	0.061
12.5	0.903	37.5	0.426	62.5	0.204	87.5	0.058
13.0	0.886	38.0	0.420	63.0	0.201	88.0	0.056
13.5	0.870	38.5	0.414	63.5	0.197	88.5	0.053
14.0	0.854	39.0	0.409	64.0	0.194	89.0	0.051
14.5	0.838	39.5	0.403	64.5	0.191	89.5	0.048
15.0	0.824	40.0	0.398	65.0	0.187	90.0	0.046
15.5	0.810	40.5	0.392	65.5	0.184	90.5	0.043
16.0	0.796	41.0	0.387	66.0	0.181	91.0	0.041
16.5	0.782	41.5	0.382	66.5	0.177	91.5	0.039
17.0	0.770	42.0	0.377	67.0	0.174	92.0	0.036
17.5	0.757	42.5	0.372	67.5	0.171	92.5	0.034
18.0	0.745	43.0	0.367	68.0	0.168	93.0	0.032
18.5	0.733	43.5	0.362	68.5	0.164	93.5	0.029
19.0	0.721	44.0	0.357	69.0	0.161	94.0	0.027
19.5	0.710	44.5	0.352	69.5	0.158	94.5	0.025
20.0	0.699	45.0	0.347	70.0	0.155	95.0	0.022
20.5	0.688	45.5	0.342	70.5	0.152	95.5	0.020
21.0	0.678	46.0	0.337	71.0	0.149	96.0	0.018
21.5	0.668	46.5	0.332	71.5	0.146	96.5	0.016
22.0	0.658	47.0	0.328	72.0	0.143	97.0	0.013
22.5	0.648	47.5	0.323	72.5	0.140	97.5	0.011
23.0	0.638	48.0	0.319	73.0	0.137	98.0	0.009
23.5	0.629	48.5	0.314	73.5	0.134	98.5	0.007
24.0	0.620	49.0	0.310	74.0	0.131	99.0	0.004
24.5	0.611	49.5	0.305	74.5	0.128	99.5	0.002
25.0	0.602	50.0	0.301	75.0	0.125	100.0	0.000
25.5	0.594	50.5	0.297	75.5	0.122		

VII. ANSWERS TO PRACTICE PROBLEM SETS AND CHAPTER REVIEW PROBLEMS

CHAPTER 1 - BASIC MATHEMATICS

PRACTICE PROBLEM SET 1.1 (Page 5)

1a. 85/100 = 17/20   d. 125/100 = 1¼
 b. 8/100 = 2/25   e. 1/400
 c. 33/200   f. 2/3

2a. 0.05   d. 0.125
 b. 0.75   e. 0.0004
 c. 0.015   f. 1.15

3a. 75%   d. 0.5%
 b. 37.5%   e. 120%
 c. 66⅔%   f. 62.5%

4a. 15%   d. 0.01%
 b. 80%   e. 33⅓%
 c. 15.5%   f. 0.05%

5. 6%$^{w/v}$ 6. 12.5%$^{v/v}$

7. 33⅓%$^{w/w}$

8. A 10%$^{w/v}$ salt solution is a solution having a ratio of 10g of salt in 100 ml total solution. A 10%$^{w/w}$ salt solution has a ratio of 10 g salt in 100 g total solution.

PRACTICE PROBLEM SET 1.2 (Page 11)

1a. 6.5×10^3 d. 1.96×10^8
 b. 2.53×10^{-3} e. 1.5×10^{-6}
 c. 1.7348×10^3 f. 3.8×10^0

2a. 0.065   e. 0.00003
 b. 41,350   f. 7.89
 c. 7020   g. 600.1
 d. 0.41

3a. 1.577×10^7 e. 7.852×10^{-5}
 b. 1.575×10^{10} f. 9.0511×10^{-4}
 c. 1.13×10^{-2} g. 5.0515×10^{-9}
 d. 3.7×10^{-1}

PRACTICE PROBLEM SET 1.3 (Page 17)

1a. 2   e. 4   i. 4
 b. 2   f. 4   j. 3
 c. 1   g. 3
 d. 4   h. 1

2a. 3500   d. 8.5
 b. 2.6   e. 90
 c. 24.9   f. 11

3. 15.26 in.   4. 62.5 g

5. 64.2 cm^2 6. 47.9 g

PRACTICE PROBLEM SET 1.4 (Page 22)

1 a. true   b. false   c. true

2a. x = 3   d. x = 40/9 = 4.44..
 b. x = 6   e. x = 32/5 = 6.4
 c. x = 2   f.   x = 2.5

3a. 30 g   d. 42 slides
 b. 3750 mg   e. 150 ml
 c. 30 g

PRACTICE PROBLEM SET 1.5 (Page 28)

1a. 2.743 m   e. 0.00003 L
 b. 0.385 kg   f.   can't be done
 c. 2300 mm   g. 8.8 ml
 d. 5.47 mg   h. 250 nl

2.   0.0225 dl   3. 1500 cl

4a. 0.386 g   b.19 mm^2 c. 3185 µg

5a. 1500 mg/L   b.   150 mg/dl

6.   brown mouse

PRACTICE PROBLEM SET 1.6 (Page 33)

1. 20.6°C   2.   378K

3. 77°F   4.   -15°C

5. -40°C   6.   -233°C

7. 10.4°F   8.   1220°F

9. -320.8°F   10.   26.7°C

CHAPTER 1 REVIEW PROBLEMS (Page 35)

1a. 12.5%   d. 20%
 b. 2.5%   e. 40%
 c. 0.5%

2a. 87.5%   b.   13.8%

3a. 1.5 g   b.   15 g

4a. 1.33×10^{-2} c. 1.25623×10^3
 b. 2.5×10^5 d. 1×10^{-9}

5a. 0.0000344   c. 0.00000000256
 b. 344,000   d. 6.0

6.   17 zeroes

7a. 4   b. 6   c. 4

8a. 6.01×10^{-3} c. 2.36×10
 b. 6.35×10^3 d. 1.70×10^{-2}

9. 2.34 g

10a. x = 125/3 = 41.66..   b.   x = 0.005

11. 550 ml   12.   4 g

13a. milligram   b. micrometer   c. centiliter

14a. larger than b. larger than   c. smaller than

15a. 6.53×10^8 ng   e. 350 m
 b. can't be done   f.   0.00012 cm
 c. 125300 g   g. 6500 ml
 d. 0.35 L   h. 65000 nm

16a. 8.58 g   c. 0.55 m^3
 b. 1.6×10^{-4} nm

17. Exact numbers occur in counting operations while approximate numbers result from measurements.

18. The precision of a measurement may be affected by the sensitivity of the measuring instrument being used and the skill of the person doing the measuring. Temperature and other environmental factors may also affect the precision of a measurement.

19. The measurement 15.0 g implies a greater degree of precision indicating that it was obtained from a more sensitive instrument than the measurement 15 g.

20. They are all the same volume.

21. 95°F   22. 31.1°C

CHAPTER 2 - DILUTIONS

PRACTICE PROBLEM SET 2.1 (Page 48)

1a. 10:5 or 2:1   b. 5:10 or 1:2
 c. 5:15 or 1:3

2. 10/45 = 2/9   3. 0.2/5 = 1/25

4. 15 ml   5. 100 ml

6. 25 ml

7. 140 ml serum ⇧ 350 ml

8. 450 ml solution; 447 ml diluent

9. 15/50 = 3/10

10. 9.5 ml diluent; 0.5/10 = 1/20

PRACTICE PROBLEM SET 2.2 (Page 52)

1. 1/50   2. 0.4 N

3. 250 mg/dl   4. 1/25

5. 0.0025%   6. 1.2%; 0.12%

7. Use 1 ml of 7.5% solution. Add enough diluent to produce total volume of 10 ml. New concentration is 0.75%

8. 1/2; 1.25 M

PRACTICE PROBLEM SET 2.4 (Page 57)

1. Tube #1: Place 2 ml of serum into a test tube and dilute up to a total volume of 10 ml using saline.
 Tube #2: Place 1 ml of serum into a test tube and dilute up to a total volume of 20 ml using saline.
 Tube #3: Place 2 ml of serum into a test tube and dilute up to a total volume of 25 ml using saline.

2.

	Tube 1	Tube 2	Tube 3
Amount of Serum	2 ml	1 ml	2 ml
Amount of Saline	8 ml	19 ml	23 ml
Total Volume	10 ml	20 ml	25 ml
Tube dilution	1/5	1/20	2/25
Solution dilution	1/5	1/20	2/25
Substance Conc.	1/5	1/20	2/25

3. Tube #1: 10 ml serum + 40 ml saline = 50 ml total
 Tube #2: 2.5 ml serum + 47.5 ml saline = 50 ml total
 Tube #3: 4 ml serum + 46 ml saline = 50 ml total

No, the concentration is unaffected since the ratio of parts has remained the same when the larger volumes were prepared.

4. Tube #1: 0.4 N
   Tube #2: 0.2 N
   Tube #3: 0.04 N

PRACTICE PROBLEM SET 2.5 (Page 64)

1. In tube #1, pipette 1 ml of serum and add enough saline to produce a total volume of 10 ml. Pipette 1 ml of solution from tube #1 into tube #2 and then add enough saline to produce a total volume of 25 ml. Pipette 1 ml of solution from tube #2 into tube #3 and add enough saline to produce a total volume of 50 ml.

   Solution Dilutions
   Tube #1: 1/10
   Tube #2: 1/250
   Tube #3: 1/12500

2. 0.4 ml urine; 99.6 ml water

3. Tube Dilution: 1/10;
   Solution Dilution: $(1/10)^3 = 1/1000$

4. 4 ml concentrate

5.

	Tube 1	Tube 2	Tube 3
Amount of Solution	1 ml	2 ml	4 ml
Amount of Diluent	9 ml	48 ml	21 ml
Total Volume	10 ml	50 ml	25 ml
Final Volume	8 ml	46 ml	25 ml
Tube Dilution	1/10	1/25	4/25
Solution Dilution	1/10	1/250	2/3125

6a. 1/5
  b. 1/5, 1/25, 1/125
  c. 1/5, 1/25, 1/125

7. 1/50; 0.1%   8. 1/100; 1/500

9.

	Tube 1	Tube 2	Tube 3
Amount of Solution	4 ml	4 ml	4 ml
Amount of Diluent	4 ml	4 ml	4 ml
Total Volume	8 ml	8 ml	8 ml
Final Volume	4 ml	4 ml	8 ml
Tube Dilution	1/2	1/2	1/2
Solution Dilution	1/2	1/4	1/8
Substance Concen.	1.25M	0.625M	0.3125M

PRACTICE PROBLEM SET 2.6 (Page 67)

1. 23 mg/dl   2. 1500 mg/dl

CHAPTER 2 REVIEW PROBLEMS (Page 69)

1a. 6/56 = 3/28   b. 6:50 or 3:25

2. 2 mg/dl   3. 200 ml

4. 0.001%

5a. Place 2 ml of serum in a test tube and add enough diluent to produce a total volume of 10 ml in that tube. Then remove 4 ml from tube #1 and place it into a second tube. Add enough diluent to the second tube to produce a total volume of 25 ml. Remove 4 ml of solution from tube #2 and place into a third tube. Add enough diluent to make a total volume of 50 ml.

  b. 6 ml; 21 ml; 50 ml

6. 3/1000; 3/10,000

7a. 0.75%   b. 12 ml
  c. solution dilution = 1/40; 39/40 of total is water

8.

	Tube 1	Tube 2	Tube 3
Amount of Solution	20 ml	10 ml	2 ml
Amount of Diluent	30 ml	40 ml	48 ml
Total Volume	50 ml	50 ml	50 ml
Final Volume	40 ml	48 ml	50 ml
Tube Dilution	2/5	1/10	1/25
Solution Dilution	2/5	1/25	1/625
Substance Concen.	2.4 N	0.24 N	0.0096 N

9. 100 ml alcohol ⇧ 250 ml; 2/5

10. 2/5   11. 12500 mg/dl

12. 1.125 N

13. yes; no; The relative concentrations of the 5% solution and diluent are the same in each tube.

14. 40,440 cells/mm³

CHAPTER 3 - SOLUTIONS

PRACTICE PROBLEM SET 3.3 (Page 82)

1. 0.3 L

2. 150 g/L; 150000 mg/L

3. 80 ml; 10%$^{w/v}$

4a. 15 g   b. 25 g   c. 3 g

5. 97.5 g NaCl + 1402.5 g H_2O

6. 4%$^{w/v}$ 7. 17.5 ml liquid soap

8. 1.25 g

9a. 4.5 g NaCl ⇧ 100 ml
 b. 4.5 g NaCl + 95.5 g H_2O

10. 200 ml

11a. 8%$^{w/v}$ b. 2.6%$^{w/v}$
 c. 1.6%$^{v/v}$ d. 1.42$^{w/w}$

12. 10 g   13. 25 g; 12.5 g

14. 12.5%$^{w/w}$ 15. 700 ml

PRACTICE PROBLEM SET 3.4 (Page 88)

1. 10 M   2. 1500 mmol

3a. 36.5 g   b. 98 g
 c. 40 g   d. 111 g

4. 250 g   5. 70.56 g

6. 7.665 g   7. 0.376 L = 376 ml

8. 4.5 M

9. 142 g Na_2SO_4 ⇧ 1000 ml

10. 292 ng   11. 0.4 M

12. 43 mmol in 1 L

13a. 175.5 g   b. 58.5 g
 c. 394.875 g   d. 1.17 g

14. 0.075 L = 75 ml

15. Use 63 g of $NaHCO_3$ and dilute up to (⇧) 500 ml producing a 1.5 M solution.

PRACTICE PROBLEM SET 3.5 (Page 94)

1a. 4 equivalents   b. 4 equivalents
 c. 4 equivalents

2. 2.4 equiv.; 2.4 equiv.   3. 1.9 N

4a. 36.5 g   b. 49 g
 c. 40 g   d. 55.5 g

5. 0.300L = 300 ml   6. 132.5 g

7. 0.04 N

8. 2.33 g $BaSO_4$ ⇧ 400 ml

9. 400 mEq   10. 1.53 N

11a.212 g   b. 70.7 g
   c.477 g   d. 1.41 g

12. 548 ml   13. 76.95 g

PRACTICE PROBLEM SET 3.6 (Page 99)

1. 49.7 g pure nitric acid

2. 242 ml of concentrated solution

3. 1.51 specific gravity

4. 10.8 M; 32.4 N

5. 15.7 M

6. 17.6 ml stock solution ⇧ 500 ml

7. 5.5 specific gravity

8. 82.9 ml of HCl solution

9. 1.24 specific gravity

10. 1 ml of concentrated solution weighs 1.65 g. Assay tells the % purity of the solution.

PRACTICE PROBLEM SET 3.7 (Page 106)

1. 300 ml   2. 187.5 ml

3. 30 ml H_2O needed   4. 60%

5. 30 ml   6. 40 ml H_2O needed

7. can't make stronger from weaker

8. 6%   9. 4.5 N

10. 20 ml of 20% saline ⇧ 100 ml

11. 2.25 N   12. 15%

13. 6.25 ml of H_2O

14. 15 ml of 15% HCl
    45 ml of 7% HCl

15. Use 62.5 ml of 12 M conc. Add enough diluent to produce 500 ml of solution. New conc. = 1.5 M

16. 62.5 ml of 2 N NaOH   17. 5 N NaOH

18. 3 N   19. 122.5 ml of H_2O

PRACTICE PROBLEM SET 3.8 (Page 115)

1. 0.26 N   2. 11.1 M; 11.1 N

3. 24%   4. 141.3 mEq/L

5. 468 mg/dl   6. 3 M H_2SO_4

7a. 6.25 mmol/L   b. 4.17 mmol/L

8. 40 ml   9. 75.98 ml = 76 ml

10. 0.18 M; 0.36 N   11. 125 ml

CHAPTER 3 REVIEW PROBLEMS (Page 117)

1. 280 ml

2a. 37.5 g   b. 50 g NaCl + 450 g H_2O

3a. 0.25%   b. 0.04 M   c. 0.04 N

4. 180 g   5. 6.7%$^{v/v}$

6. 16 ml alcohol ⇧ 200 ml

7. can't be done   8. 4125 ml H_2O

9. 6 N

10. 187.5 ml of 20%   11. 30 ml of 6 N
   312.5 ml of 12%   70 ml of 4 N

12a. 2.5 moles solute/L; 245 g
  b. 250 mEq/L; 0.25 mEq/L

13. 14.3 M   14. 84 g

15. 4 M   16. 1306 ng

17. 0.3 N

18a. 625 mEq   b. 34.6875 g

19. 27.375 g HCl ⇧ 500 ml

20a. 0.19 M   b. 0.38 N   c. 2%$^{w/v}$

21a. 20%$^{v/v}$ b. 35.1%$^{w/v}$
  c. 3.6 M   d. 7.2 N

22. 365 ml HNO_3 ⇧ 1 L

23a. 2.6 M   b. 44%$^{w/v}$

24a. 4.3 mEq/L   b. 4.3 mmol/L

25. 30 ml

26a. 2827.5 mg/dl   b. 725 mmol/L   c. 0.725 N

CHAPTER 4 - LOGARITHMS, pH AND IONIC SOLUTIONS

PRACTICE PROBLEM SET 4.2A (Page 128)

1. $\log_{10} 75 = x$ 2. $\log_5 x = 2$

3. $\log_e 42.4 = x$ 4. $\log_x 500 = 5$

5. $\log_{10} x = 3$ 6. $\log_e x = 1/2$

7. $\log_x B = a$ 8. $\log_{169} x = 1/2$

9. $\log_{10} x = -4$ 10. $\log_e (2/3) = x$

11. $\log_3 9 = 2$ 12. $\log_{(-3)} (-27) = 3$

13. $\log_{10} 1000 = 3$ 14. $\log_e 1 = 0$

15. $\log_{1/2} (1/8) = 3$

PRACTICE PROBLEM SET 4.2B (Page 128)

1. $5^x = 25$ 2. $10^2 = x$

3. $(-3)^{1x} = -8$ 4. $x^4 = 3.65$

5. $x^c = A$ 6. $(1/2)^{20} = x$

7. $e^x = 40$ 8. $e^{2.49} = x$

9. $10^x = 2$ 10. $2^9 = x$

11. $10^2 = 100$ 12. $e^1 = 2.71828$

13. $5^3 = 125$ 14. $2^5 = 32$

15. $400^{1/2} = 20$

PRACTICE PROBLEM SET 4.3 (Page 132)

1. 2   2. 3

3. 1.3979   4. 0.6628

5. undefined   6. -1.3098

7. 4.6990   8. 0.4077

9. -0.3010   10. 0.5378

PRACTICE PROBLEM SET 4.4 (Page 134)

1. 4.6052   2. 1.6094

3. 1.0260   4. undefined

5. 1   6. undefined

7. -5.3475   8. 9.9035

9. -1.3863   10. 0

PRACTICE PROBLEM SET 4.5 (Page 137)

1. 10 000   2. 0.0001

3. 1.2840   4. 4.6416

5. 190.5663   6. 0.9120

7. 3.4277   8. 7.3891

9. 0.7047   10. 1000

PRACTICE PROBLEM SET 4.7 (Page 143)

1. 11   2. 7.7

3. 1.3

4a. 0.3 mol H^+/L   b. 0.52
 c. 13.48   d. 3.33 X 10^{-14} mol OH^-/L

5. 0.19g   6. 7

7.   1 X 10^{-6} mol H^+/L

8. 7.75

9.   1.78 X 10^{-5} mol H^+/L

10a.4.38   b. 2.38 X 10^{-10} mol OH^-/L

PRACTICE PROBLEM SET 4.9 (Page 149)

1. 6.00   2. 5.50

3. pH = pK   4. pH = pK

5. 48.98 g sodium acetate + 0.16 g acetic acid ⇧
    1000ml ⇨ 1L of 0.6 N acetate buffer solution

CHAPTER 4 REVIEW PROBLEMS (Page 151)

1a. 1.3010   b. 2.9957
 c. 305.9849   d. undefined

2a. 9   b. -2   c. 0.2

3. 4.38   4. 2.38 X10^{-10}

5. 8.8, basic   6. 1.7783 X 10^{-6}

7a. 0.375 g H^+/L   b. 2.67 X 10^{-14} g OH^-/L
 c. 0.4260   d. 13.5740

8. 6.62

9. 0.08 g NaOH ⇧ 200 ml ⇨ 200 ml NaOH
    solution·(pH = 12)

10. 15.3 g sodium acetate + 0.101 g acetic acid ⇧
    250 ml ⇨ 250 ml of 0.75 N acetate buffer

CHAPTER 5- GRAPHS AND GRAPHING

PRACTICE PROBLEM SET 5.2 (Page 165)

1. y-int = (0,1); x-int = (-1,0); y = 16 when x = 15

2a. P = 90   b. T = 80
  d. x-int = (-320,0); y-int = (0,80)

3. case E

4. x-int = (1,0); y-int = none

5. concentration = 6.8 when A = 0.678

6. %T = 20% when concentration = 6.9

PRACTICE PROBLEM SET 5.3 (Page 172)

1. semi-log   2. rectangular

3. rectangular   4. semi-log

5. rectangular

6. single cycle semilog, st. line

7. 5+ cycle semilog, st. line

8. 3+ cycle semilog, st. line

9. 4+ cycle semilog, st. line

10. 4 cycle semilog, st. line

11. 2 cycle semilog, st. line

PRACTICE PROBLEM SET 5.4 (Page 179)

1a. graph on single cycle semilog paper
  b. concentration = 6.8 when %T = 21%
  c. concentration = 6.9
  d. % difference = 1.4%
e(b). concentration = 7.6 when %T = 17%
e(c). concentration = 7.8
e(d). % difference = 2.6%

2. graph on rect. paper; concentration = 6.6 when A = 0.482

3a. single cycle semilog graph, concentration = 3×10^{-10}
  b. less than 10%

4. 0.1549, 0.3391, 0.5157, 0.7122, 0.9031

5. 2.999%, 29.99%, 76.03%, 84.53%, 1%

CHAPTER 5 REVIEW PROBLEMS (Page 182)

1a. rect. graph paper
  b. mileage = 27.8 mpg
  c. slope = 28.7 mpg

2. 109 mg/ml   3. 77.1 ml/L

4. single cycle semilog graph; concentration = 6.58

5. rectangular graph paper; concentration = 3.5

CHAPTER 6 - THE MATHEMATICS OF BLOOD COUNTS

PRACTICE PROBLEM SET 6.4 (Page 195)

1a. 1/20   b. 1/10

2a. 1/200   b. 1/100

3. 6.8×10^6 cells/ml
    6.8×10^9 cells/L

4. 3.75×10^7 cells/ml   5. 4.4×10^6 cells/mm³

6. 15   7. 1.225×10^{10} cells/L

PRACTICE PROBLEM SET 6.5 (Page199)

	MCV	MCH	MCHC
1.	90.9 μm³	27.3 pg	30%
2.	93.0 μm³	26.7 pg	28.8%
3.	100 μm³	20.8 pg	20.8%
4.	105.6 μm³	15 pg	14.2%
5.	71.1 μm³	23.1 pg	32.5%

CHAPTER 6 REVIEW PROBLEMS (Page 201)

1a. 5000 cells/mm³   b. 5×10^9 cells/L

2. 17   3. 2.35×10^6 cells/μL

4. 11250 cells/μL

5a. MCV = 90 μm³   b. MCV = 64.6 μm³
    MCH = 28 pg   MCH = 18.9 pg
    MCHC = 31.1%   MCHC = 29.3%

6a. 2.5×10^6 cells/ml   b. 2.5×10^9 cells/L

7. 3.2×10^6 RBC/μL   8. 3.9×10^6 WBC/ml

9. 30.3%

CHAPTER 7: STATISTICS AND QUALITY CONTROL

PRACTICE PROBLEM SET 7.1 (Page 206)

1A) qualitative   B) nominal

2A) quantitative   B) ratio

3A) quantitative   B) interval

4A) quantitative   B) ratio

5A) quantitative   B) ratio

6A) qualitative   B) ordinal

7A) quantitative   B) ratio

8A) qualitative   B) nominal

9A) quantitative   B) interval

10A) quantitative   B) ratio

11A) quantitative   B) ratio

12A) qualitative   B) ordinal

13A) qualitative   B) nominal

PRACTICE PROBLEM SET 7.2 (Page 212)

1a) mean = 7.1   median = 6.5   mode = 5
 b) mean = 458.4   median = 516   mode = none
 c) mean = 7.34   median = 6.75   mode = 5.6

2. mode only   3. 376 per year

4. The median, due to the two 'extremely' small numbers.

5. 3.8 ml/hr

PRACTICE PROBLEM SET 7.3 (Page 217)

1. R = 42   s = 13.7

2. R = 3.6   s = 1.26

3. The numbers are all identical.

4. The numbers are all identical.

5. CV - 4.2%

PRACTICE PROBLEM SET 7.5 (Page 231)

1.   rules 1-2S and 2-2S
2a. rule 1-2S   c. rule 10x
 b. none   d. none, but the <u>long</u> trend upwards should be watched

3a. 50%   c. 15.74%
 b. 81.85%   d. 15.74%

CHAPTER 7 REVIEW PROBLEMS (Page 234)

1. A population is <u>all</u> possible data where as a sample is just a partial data set.

2. Quantitative data is a set of measurements or amounts (generally numbers). Qualitative data is a set of attributes or qualities (not generally numerical in nature.)

3. The level of data determines what statistical analysis is valid for the data in question.

4. Descriptive statistics deals with the actual data collected and the organization and calculation done with it. Inferential statistics takes the know information and uses it to make generalizations, estimations, etc. In problem set 7.5 problem number 3, you were inferring some information from the fact that the data was normally distributed.

5. qualitative, nominal

6. quantitative, ratio   7. quantitative, ratio

8. quantitative, interval

9. mean = 7.1 ml
    median = 7.1 ml
    mode = 7.2 ml
    'Best' average is the mean here.

10. mean = 6.6
    median = 3
    mode = 2
    "Best average here is the median.

11. mean = none
    median = none
    mode = blue

BIBLIOGRAPHY

Clinical Chemistry - Concepts and Applications, Shauna C. Anderson and Susan Cockayne, W.B.Saunders Company, Harcourt Brace Jovanovich, Inc. Philadelphia, Penn., 1993.

Clinical Hematology and Fundamentals of Hemostasis, 2nd Ed. Denise M. Harmening, F.A.Davis Company, Philadelphia,1992.

Clinical Hematology Principles, Procedures, Correlations, Lotspeich-Steininger, Cheryl A., J.B. Lippincott Co., Philadelphia, 1992.

Clinical Hematology - Theory and Practice, Mary Louise Turgeon, Little, Brown and Co., Boston/Toronto, 1988.

Foundations of College Chemistry, Morris Hein and Susan Arena, Brooks/Cole Publishing Co., Pacific Grove, Cal., 1993.

Laboratory Mathematics, June Campbell and Joe B. Campbell, C. V. Mosby, St. Louis, Missouri, 1990.

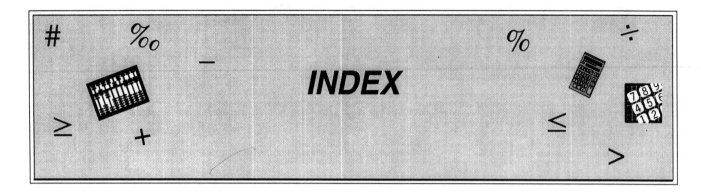

A

Absorbance (A) 174
Absorptivity coefficient 174
Acids 138
Antilog 135
Approximate 12
Assay 96
Avagadro's number 84
Averages 207
Axes 158

B

Bases 138
Beer's Law 73, 174
Bell curve 218
Buffer 144

C

Calculator 238
Coefficient of variation (CV) 215
Colorimetry 173
Common ion effect 145
Common logs 129
Concentration 3, 49, 60, 76
Control limits 224
Conversion 108
Conversion factor 24
Cuvette 173
Cycle 169

D

Data 204
Degree of dissociation 144
Density 96
Dependent dilution series 58
Dependent variable 158
Descriptive statistics 204
Diluted up to (⇧) 79
Diluting up 45

Dilution 44
Dilution correction factor 66
Dilution factor 188
Dilution ratio 44, 49
Dilution series 54
Directly proportional 163
Dispersion 213
Dissociate 138

E

e 133
Equivalent weight 90
Equivalents 90
Exact 12
Exponent 124
Exponential form 125
Extrapolation 166

F

Final Volume 53
Fold 62
Frequency 218
Frequency distribution 218

H

Hemacytometer 186
Henderson-Hasselbalch relationship 144

I

Imprecision 225
Independent 54
Independent dilution 54
Independent variable 158
Inferential statistics 204
Intercepts 166
Interval level data 205
Inversely proportional 163
Ionize 138

OTHER PUBLICATIONS FROM SKIDMORE-ROTH PUBLISHING, INC.

INSTANT INSTRUCTOR SERIES	code	isbn #	price	qty
AIDS	ADIN01	1-56930-010-0	$ 16.95	
C.C.U.	CCINC1	1-56930-022-4	$ 16.95	
Diabetes	DBII01	1-56930-041-0	$ 16.95	
Geriatric	GRN01	0-944132-68-5	$ 16.95	
Hemodialysis	DLIN01	1-56930-020-8	$ 16.95	
I.C.U.	ICUI01	1-56930-021-6	$ 16.95	
IV, Krasner	IVII01	1-56930-043-7	$ 16.95	
Lab, Stauffer	LBIN01	0-944132-70-7	$ 16.95	
Obstetric	OBIN01	0-944132-67-7	$ 16.95	
Oncology	ONIN01	1-56930-023-2	$ 16.95	
Pediatric	PDIN01	0-944132-66-9	$ 16.95	
NURSING CARE PLANS SERIES				
AIDS	ADSC01	0-56930-000-3	$ 36.95	
Critical Care	CNCP01	1-56930-035-6	$ 36.95	
Geriatric (2nd ed.)	GNCP02	1-56930-052-6	$ 36.95	
Oncology	ONCP01	1-56930-004-6	$ 36.95	
Pediatric (2nd ed.)	PNOP02	1-56930-057-7	$ 36.95	
NURSE'S SURVIVAL GUIDE SERIES				
Geriatric Nurse's Survival Guide	GSGD01	1-56930-061-5	$ 29.95	
Nurse's Survival Guide (2nd ed.)	NSGD02	0-944132-75-8	$ 32.95	
Obstetric Survival Guide	OBSG01	0-944132-94-4	$ 29.95	
Pediatric Survival Guide	PNGD01	1-56930-018-6	$ 29.95	
NURSING/OTHER				
Body In Brief (3rd ed.)	BBRF03	1-56930-055-0	$ 35.95	
Diagnostic and Lab Cards (2nd ed.)	DLC02	0-944132-77-4	$ 27.95	
Drug Comparison Handbook (2nd ed.)	DRUG02	1-56930-16-x	$ 35.95	
Essential Laboratory Mathematics	ELM01	1-56930-056-9	$ 29.95	
Geriatric Long-Term Procedures & Treatments (2nd ed.)	GLTP02	1-56930-072-0	$ 34.95	
Geriatric Nutrition and Diet (2nd ed.)	NUT02	1-56930-045-3	$ 17.95	
Handbook of Long Term Care (2nd ed.)	HLTC02	1-56930-058-5	$ 22.95	
Handbook For Nurse Assistants (2nd ed.)	HNA02	1-56930-059-3	$ 19.95	
I.C.U. Quick Reference	ICQU01	1-56930-003-8	$ 32.95	
Infection Control	INFC01	1-56930-051-8	$ 94.95	
Nursing Diagnosis Cards (2nd ed.)	NDC02	1-56930-060-7	$ 29.95	
Nurse's Trivia Calendar	NTC98	1-56930-073-9	$ 11.95	
OBRA (2nd ed.)	OBRA02	1-56930-046-1	$ 99.95	
OSHA Book (2nd ed.)	OSHA	1-56930-069-0	$ 119.95	
Procedure Cards (3rd ed.)	PCCU03	1-56930-054-2	$ 24.95	
Pharmacy Tech	PHAR01	1-56930-005-4	$ 25.95	
Spanish For Medical Personnel	SPAN01	1-56930-001-1	$ 21.95	
Staff Develop. For the Psych. Nurse	STDEV0	0-944132-78-2	$ 59.95	

OUTLINE SERIES	code	isbn #	price	qty
Diabetes Outline	DBOL01	1-56930-031-3	$ 22.95	
Fundamentals of Nursing Outline	FUND01	1-56930-029-1	$ 22.95	
Geriatric Outline	GER01	1-56930-050-x	$ 22.95	
Hemodynamic Monitoring Outline	HDMO01	1-56930-034-8	$ 22.95	
High Acuity Outline	HATO01	1-56930-028-3	$ 22.95	
Med-Surgical Nursing Outline (2nd ed.)	MSN02	1-56930-068-2	$ 22.95	
Obstetric Nursing Outline (2nd ed.)	OBS02	1-56930-070-4	$ 22.95	
Pediatric Nursing Outline	PN01	0-944132-89-8	$ 22.95	
RN NCLEX REVIEW SERIES				
Concepts of Medical Surgical Nursing	NMS01	0-944132-85-5	$ 21.95	
Concepts of Obstetric Nursing	NOB01	0-944132-86-3	$ 21.95	
Concepts of Psychiatric Nursing	NPSY01	0-944132-83-9	$ 21.95	
PN/VN Review Cards (2nd ed.)	PNRC02	1-56930-008-9	$ 29.95	
RN Review Cards (2nd ed.)	RNRC02	0-944132-82-0	$ 29.95	

Name _____

Address _____

City _____ State _____ Zip _____

Phone ( ) _____

❑ VISA   ❑ MasterCard   ❑ American Express   ❑ Check/Money Order

Card # _____ Expiration Date _____

Signature (required) _____

Prices subject to change. Please add $6.95 each, for postage and handling. Include your local sales tax.

MAIL OR FAX ORDER TO:
  SKIDMORE-ROTH PUBLISHING, INC.
  2620 S. Parker Road, Suite 147
  Aurora, Colorado 80014
  1 (800) 825-3150   FAX (303) 306-1460

Visit our website at: http://www.skidmore-roth.com